# Inspiring

*to live*

# Breakthrough

*your dreams*

# Secrets

Susan A. Friedmann, CSP • Yael Friedmann • Betty J. Pyykola • Toni Ann Robino

Patrick Snow • Dr. Riccardo J. Cifola • Robert Mari • Dr. Amelia Case • Lillian Zarzar

Dr. Esther Konigsberg • Karrin Ochoa • Christine K. Clifford • Mark A. Lorenson

# Inspiring
*to live*
# Breakthrough
*your dreams*
# Secrets

Compiled by
**Susan A. Friedmann, CSP**

Edited by: Toni Ann Robino,
With Flying Colours, Junction City, OH

Cover Design by Kathiann Tevlin,
In the Woods Design Studio,
Lake Placid, NY

Page Layout by: Ad Graphics, Inc., Tulsa, OK

Printed in the United States of America

Library of Congress Catalog Number 2001094638

ISBN  1-890427-08-X

Published by:

a subsidiary of
**Diadem Communications**
P.O. Box 1850
Lake Placid, NY  12946-5850


Additional copies of
*Inspiring Breakthrough Secrets to Live Your Dreams*
can be obtained from any of the authors by calling
their individual number as listed with their chapter.




Quantity discounts are available.

# CONTENTS

# FOREWORD

What if you walked into a bookstore, silently followed your intuition, and were mysteriously led to the perfect book? What if that book were right here and now? If you are reading these lines, it is not an accident or a coincidence, for you are about to discover that your intuition has wisely led you to a magical book.

What if this special book were filled with morsels of wisdom that could help you fulfill your heart and soul's desires? Would you become inspired if this were true? Would you continue reading further and discover why and for what purpose you were led to this very special place and time? I hope so, for you have just entered a world where magical transformations are about to take place, where dreams are about to be brought into reality, and where destinies are about to be fulfilled. Welcome to the world of *Inspiring Breakthrough Secrets to Live Your Dreams.*

Nuggets of golden wisdom come in many forms and are extracted from many hidden places. Imagine what would happen if you met a group of modern day heroes who revealed powerful words which transformed your misfortunes into fortunes and your crises into blessings. What if their secrets could guide you gently to your destiny?

Whether you are a child or an adult, a man or a woman, this enlightening book, filled with the wisdom of such heroes, will help you see that nothing is missing in your present earthly existence. With the guidance of these authors, you can become attuned with the inner music of the cosmos, experience quantum jumps in your consciousness, and awaken to the heightened awareness of your marvelous and hidden inner balance.

This book was written from the inner selves of a special group of heroic muses committed to unveiling your true inner being. You were destined to come into the presence of such masters, and it is they who, in turn, will help you to manifest the greatness you deserve and assist you in sharing ever-greater and loving service with others. I now introduce you to your magnificent and hidden destiny through this magical book, *Inspiring Breakthrough Secrets to Live Your Dreams.*

**Dr. John F. Demartini**
International speaker, consultant.
Best-selling author of *Count Your Blessings:
the Healing Power of Gratitude and Love.*
Founder of the *Concourse of Wisdom School.*
Originator of *The Breakthrough Experience*™ and
*The Quantum Collapse Process.*™
www.drdemartini.com

# INTRODUCTION

Inspiration is the catalyst that brings dreams to life. When we're inspired, we can run faster, jump higher, spread our wings, and fly!

There are many valuable secrets that can help you to live your dreams, but the secrets that kindle the flames of your inspiration are priceless. The secrets shared by the authors in this book will touch the heights and depths of your mind, heart, and soul. Each of the twelve specialized chapters is a guidepost along the path to your dreams. Each author offers insights, strategies, or transformational tools that can empower you to turn your dreams into reality.

If you're already living your dreams, this powerful book will open up a whole new world of possibilities. If you yearn to live your dreams, but don't know where or how to begin, you're in the right place.

If you can dream it, you can live it!

**Susan A. Friedmann, CSP**
Diadem Communications
Lake Placid, NY

# CHAPTER ONE

# Go to the Moon Without a Rocket!

*by*
*Toni Ann Robino*

# Go to the Moon Without a Rocket!

Toni Ann Robino

---

*"Nothing happens unless first a dream."*

– Carl Sandburg

---

**Y**ou *can* live your dreams. In fact, at this very moment, whether you realize it or not, you already have the capacity to follow the dreams in your heart. You are not given inspirations unless you possess the power to pursue them.

So why do most people turn away from following their inspirations? One reason is because they just don't believe they can achieve their dreams. Some give up before they ever try. Others throw in the towel when they meet opportunities cleverly disguised as difficulties. What's ironic, is that this line of reasoning blinds them to one of the most essential secrets to manifesting their visions. The secret is this: It's not the *achievement* of a dream that brings fulfillment and meaning to our lives; it's everything that occurs in the *process* of our pursuit.

When you're following the path of an inspired dream, your life is filled with interesting discoveries, exciting events, and endless possibilities. The energy of your enthusiasm is magnetic and you actually attract the people, resources, and circumstances that can assist you. You also attract challenges and hurdles. Thank God! Because as the proverb says, "Smooth seas do not make skillful sailors." Every time you solve a problem, turn a challenge into an opportunity, or jump a hurdle, you break through to a greater level of certainty and your self-worth increases.

Just as necessity breeds invention, challenges allow you to find out how capable and powerful you really are. Rather than despair at your trials and tribulations, make them your allies and use them to become stronger, wiser, and more centered in your own truth.

# Trust Your Truth

*"Your dream will become clear*
*only when you can look into your own heart.*
*Who looks outside, dreams; who looks inside, awakes."*

– Carl Jung

If you open your heart and look deep inside, you will find your dreams. They are waiting for you to acknowledge them and bring them to life. But acknowledging them isn't enough. Once you've awakened your dreams, it's essential that you nurture them.

Dreams blossom with your attention, gratitude, and willingness to trust your own truth. Your truth is the perfect reflection of your highest inspirations. It's the wisdom of your soul. No one knows the path of your soul, convictions of your mind, or the depth of your heart better than you do. After all, how could they? You, and you alone, are privy to your ongoing stream of thoughts, feelings, and intuitions. That means that where your inspirations are concerned, *you* are the expert.

Everyone has dreams they would love to pursue, but many people run their lives according to what they think others expect from them. Some are seeking praise or approval; others are trying to avoid rejection or reprimand. Don't get caught in the tangled web of living your life based on other people's beliefs, values, or priorities! If others' opinions of you and your dream are more important to you than your own, it is *essential* that you learn to trust your own truth.

You can do this by listening to the voice within that whispers and sometimes shouts guidance. The more you listen to this inner voice, the more clearly you will hear it. In a sense, you are exercising the pathways of communication between your heart, mind, and soul. The more you use these pathways, the easier it will be to tune into and listen to your soul's messages. By following this inspired guidance, you will learn — by experience — that you *can* and *do* trust your own truth.

The more firmly you are centered in your truth, the more powerfully you can move toward your dreams. Once you are grounded and balanced in your own wisdom, you will not be so easily swayed by the currents around you. You will also learn how to draw strength from yourself, and in doing so, you will discover aspects of yourself that you may not know you possess.

### Ten Steps to Trusting Your Truth

This exercise is designed to assist you in learning to still your mind and open your heart to the truth of your soul. The more often you practice this method, the more clearly you will hear this guidance and the sooner you will learn to trust your truth.

1.  Select a question that you would like to ask your soul.

2.  Sit in a comfortable chair, close your eyes, and breathe through your nose. Balance your breathing. (If you inhale for seven seconds, exhale for seven seconds) Do this for at least one full minute to settle into a rhythm.

3.  Silently hold your question in your mind as you continue your rhythmic breathing.

4.  Imagine that you can see the image of your soul on a life-size screen in front of you. Imagine that your soul looks just like you, only it is brighter, as if it's giving off light.

5.  Take a few minutes to silently thank all of the people who have played a part in making you who you are today.

6.  When your heart opens with gratitude, ask your soul the question that you have formulated.

7.  Listen carefully to everything your soul says. If you're confused by something, ask for clarification.

8.  Thank your soul for its love and wisdom and let the image fade away. If the answer did not come during this exercise, trust that it will soon be revealed to you.

9.  Open your eyes, and before speaking with anyone, write down everything your soul said.

10. Follow the inspired guidance that you have received.

# Believe in Your Dreams

*"The future belongs to those who*
*believe in the beauty of their dreams."*

– Eleanor Roosevelt

Ever since I was a little girl my mother has told me, "You can go to the moon without a rocket!" These words have found a special place in my heart because they affirm what I now know to be true. The only limitations we have in life are those we agree to go along with. If we refuse to be limited, and keep looking, we eventually find a way. What we believe is in direct alignment with what we achieve.

Think about it. How many times have you achieved something that you didn't believe you could accomplish? Perhaps you've received a few gifts along the way, but overall, your accomplishments follow your beliefs. To believe that you can go to the moon without a rocket is to acknowledge that you have the power to pursue your dreams — whatever they are and wherever they may lead. You are giving yourself permission to follow your inspired path and you're calling upon your inner strength and wisdom to assist you. Many of the forces that can help you to follow your inspirations lie dormant until you awaken them with your belief. That's one of the reasons believing in your dreams is so important. If the path you're on seems to have hit a dead end, take a step back and look for your options.

Let me share an example. When I decided that I wanted to go to college, I had several hurdles to jump. For one thing, I was enrolled in my high school's business track, rather than in the college preparatory track. That meant I didn't have the necessary requirements for college entry. I also didn't have the best grades, often putting more time into extracurricular activities than my homework, and my college entrance exam scores were far from stellar. The deck appeared to be stacked against me, but I was determined and believed that I could find a way.

I put all my "shortcomings" on the shelf and began looking at college catalogs. Once I selected the university I wanted to attend, I investigated their enrollment requirements and procedures. What I lacked in requirements was compensated for by what I learned about the enrollment process. The university I chose accepted students based on the college in which they applied. I wanted to major in journalism, but I learned that the College of Journalism received twice as many applicants as they could accommodate. I also discovered that enrollment in the College of English was very low and sliding. I knew that once I was enrolled in the university I could change my major, so I applied to the College of English and was quickly accepted. I wasn't breaking the rules, I was simply making them work for me. You can do this too!

When you fortify your belief in your dreams, your conscious and subconscious mind team up to chart a course that will work for you. Your belief gives you courage when you face doubts and fears, and it lifts you up when you feel down or discouraged. In a very real sense, your belief is the shining star that can light your path through night and day, calm and storm.

## *Fortifying Your Belief in Your Dreams*

1.   Write down an inspired dream that you hold in your heart. (Be very clear and precise.)

2.   Write the question, "Why don't I believe I can pursue this dream?"

3.   List and number all of the reasons that you don't believe you can follow this inspiration.

4.   For each obstacle you listed in #3, write 3 to 5 ways that you can overcome or surmount it.

5.   Write the question, "Why do I believe I *can* pursue this dream?"

6.   Write as many reasons why you *can* pursue this dream as you listed for why you can't. Then write 10 more.

7.   Close your eyes and imagine yourself living this dream. Visualize it in vivid detail. Incorporate all of your senses. Bring this dream to life in your virtual reality and experience the energy, fulfillment, and power that pursuing and living your dream awakens in you.

# Prepare for Lift-off

*"And I have the firm belief in this now, not only in terms of my own experience, but in knowing about the experience of others, that when you follow your bliss, doors will open where you would not have thought there were going to be doors, and where there wouldn't be a door for anybody else."*

– Joseph Campbell

By trusting your truth, you are able to build the rocket ship to your dreams. The amount of belief you have in your inspirations is equal to the amount of fuel you have for your journey. Taking action on your dreams is what gives you the extra power and confidence to lift off.

Begin by taking just one step, and then take another and another and another. With each step you take, your belief that you can live your dreams will increase. Through taking action, your belief will eventually transform into a sense of "knowing." Once you *know* that you can live your dreams, the whole world opens up. The catch is that you won't know that you can do something until you do it. The certainty of "knowing" is a level beyond belief and it generally comes from your own experience.

For example, do you remember how you felt before you learned how to ride a bicycle? Your belief that you could do it encouraged you to give it a try. But your confidence came when you rode that first stretch of road all by yourself. At that magical moment, your belief was transformed into knowledge.

Keep in mind that you probably didn't hop onto the bike and smoothly take off the first time. In my case, my dad ran up our road holding the back of my purple Huffy for at least a half-mile before I agreed to try it myself. It was wobbly and scary at first, but with each driveway I passed, my belief in my ability increased. My dad helped me to believe I could do it, and once I knew it was true, there was no stopping me.

When you act on your inspirations it works the same way. Each step you take toward your dreams helps you to build confidence and increases your momentum. And by the way, *there are no small steps*. Even the minutest movement in the direction of your dreams will shift your path to one that is more meaningful and fulfilling for you.

The bridge between belief and certainty is built with experience. If you're waiting until you know you can do something before you're willing to try it, you're allowing doubt or fear to stop you in your tracks. Wouldn't it be more rewarding to learn by experience that you're already powerful enough to begin and wise enough to learn along the way?

For instance, the first time I was asked to write a book, I believed I could do it, so I accepted the offer. I was ecstatic about the opportunity and walking on air. Then the contract arrived and the reality set in. As I signed my name, my hand began to shake, my mouth went dry, and I was gripped with anxiety. My "monkey mind" began taunting me with "You can't write a book! Why did you ever say you could do it? Now look what you've gotten yourself into!" The fear didn't subside until I sat down at the computer and began to write. Each time monkey mind piped up to discourage me, I made a beeline for the computer and I wrote. Every sentence that I typed affirmed my belief that I could do it. But it wasn't until I completed the first chapter that I *knew* I could write the entire book. It was at that moment that I experienced a level of certainty and fulfillment that I had never experienced before.

The power of "knowing" increases your energy level, lifts your heart, and awakens you to greater possibilities. You can quiet your monkey mind and transform your belief into knowledge by keeping your dreams in sight and putting one foot in front of the other. I can't overemphasize the value and importance of continually taking action steps. Even a step in the so-called "wrong" direction will lead you to an understanding that you didn't have before. There really are no mistakes, so every inspired step is worth taking.

One of the secrets to successfully moving forward lies in the old adage, "Where there's a will, there's a way." Your inspired will can unlock doors and illuminate the darkest passageways. When you commit to following your dream, you are inspired to ask quality questions, tune into opportunities, and chart new territory. When you decide that giving up is not an option, a deluge of viable options present themselves to you.

## *Transforming Beliefs into Knowledge*

1.  Take a moment to reflect on one of your inspired dreams. (You may want to continue working with the one you wrote down in the exercise *Fortifying Your Belief in Your Dream*.)

2.  Write one action step that you can take right now to pursue this dream. (Remember there are no small steps. It might be reading a page of a book, making a phone call, or updating part of your resume.)

3.  Put this action step on your calendar for tomorrow and commit to accomplishing it before the day ends.

4.  Repeat this process daily for the rest of your life. (I'm not kidding! Of course you can take a day off here and there, but your greatest fulfillment in life is derived through the pursuit of your dreams. Why limit yourself to taking action steps *occasionally*, when you can experience the magic of your inspirations *every day*?)

You *can* go to the moon without a rocket! You can pursue anything your heart desires. The path to your dreams is your calling and your birthright. By following this path, your life is guaranteed to be filled with exactly what is most valuable for your growth and evolution. Remember that achieving your dreams is just one small part of the journey. Resist the urge to place more importance on the accomplishment than on the path itself.

Every day the world offers you something valuable. Every twist and turn along your path presents a new view. Learn to treasure each opportunity, event, person, and obstacle that you encounter. If it's on your path, it's part of your journey. (There's no getting around this one.)

The more you align your thoughts and actions with your inspirations, the more you will appreciate each day and the more meaningful and fulfilling your life will become. When your dreams direct your life, your life reflects your dreams. This is the magic of manifestation. This is the secret to living your dreams.

\* \* \* \* \* \* \*

In Chapter Two, discover the secret of powerful words and affirmations.

# About Toni Ann Robino

**T**oni Ann Robino inspires individuals and organizations to define, clarify, and achieve their personal and professional dreams for success. She is a consultant, author, editor, and professional speaker. Her knowledge and experience in personal and professional development, interpersonal communication, philosophy, psychology, and natural health combine to form the foundation for her courses, articles, and books.

Toni Ann and her husband, Steven Lee Barker, created With Flying Colours in 1991 to encourage individuals, organizations, and businesses to *Dare to Reach their Highest Dreams*. With Flying Colours offers a variety of presentations, seminars, and workshops, including "Wisdom of the Woods," "Two Hearts Dancing," and "Book-Walk," a unique book-writing workshop.

She also teaches *The Breakthrough Experience*™, a cutting-edge personal and professional development seminar created by Dr. John F. Demartini, founder of The Concourse of Wisdom School of Philosophy and Healing. Through this work, she has guided thousands of people worldwide to discover more of their own magnificence, listen to their inner wisdom, and live their dreams. She received the Ambassador of Wisdom Award from The Concourse of Wisdom "in honor of an extra-special emissary service that expands the outreach of love and wisdom throughout the world."

Toni Ann is the editor and co-author of *Breakthrough Secrets to Live Your Dreams*, and the editor of *Count Your Blessings: The Healing Power of Gratitude and Love*, by Dr. John F. Demartini, now available in nine languages. She is also the co-author of *Make Up, Don't Break Up, Finding and Keeping Love for Singles and Couples*.

# With Flying Colours
## ~ *Dare to reach your highest dreams* ~

Box 371 Junction City, Ohio 43748
Phone: 740-987-6873 • Fax: 740-987-8709

Email: Robino@WithFlyingColours.com
Website: www.WithFlyingColours.com

## Services:

➤ Private and Group Consultations

➤ Personalized Success Programs for Individuals and Couples

➤ Custom-Designed Workshops and Seminars for Businesses and Organizations

## Seminars Include:

**The Breakthrough Experience™**

Break through obstacles and limitations in *all* areas of life. Uncover your own magnificence. Discover your inspired purpose in life. Experience The Quantum Collapse Process™ and transform "problems" into the powerful energy of gratitude and love.

**Book-Walk**

This one-of-a-kind course provides all of the tools you need to turn your dream to write a book — into a book! Whether you're a published writer, or dream of becoming one, Book-Walk leads you step-by-step through the process of writing your book, from concept through publication.

You'll learn the ups and downs of "being published" versus "self-publishing," and receive savvy advice from some of America's leading literary agents and publicists. Most importantly, you'll learn a transformational process that gives you the creative energy and insight to leap over "authors' roadblocks" — whether those obstacles are time constraints, financial concerns, family or career challenges, or your own doubts or fears. Book-Walk includes four group sessions and one-on-one coaching with Toni Ann Robino.

**Wisdom of the Woods**

*When we reconnect with nature, we remember who we are.*

During this weekend workshop:

➤ Experience the ancient wisdom found in the elements of nature.

➤ Receive inspired messages from your heart and soul.

➤ Learn about edible and medicinal plants and trees.

➤ Follow your intuition to find sacred signs, tokens, and insights during a silent vision quest.

➤ Spark inspired visions for your future.

# Books Include:

*Breakthrough Secrets to Live Your Dreams.* Co-authored and edited by Toni Ann Robino. Available through With Flying Colours.

*Restocking Your Medicine Cabinet with Nature's Healing Treasures* by Toni Ann Robino. Available through With Flying Colours.

*Make Up, Don't Break Up; Finding and Keeping Love for Singles and Couples* by Dr. Bonnie Eaker Weil with Toni Robino. Available in bookstores and on-line at Amazon.com

For more information, contact Toni Ann Robino at With Flying Colours.

# CHAPTER TWO

# Powerful Words – Affirmations

*by*
*Dr. Riccardo J. Cifola*

# Powerful Words – Affirmations

Dr. Riccardo J. Cifola

---

*"Without knowing the force of words,*
*it is impossible to know men."*

– Confucius

---

The power of words can not be underestimated. Whether you are talking to yourself, or communicating with others, words are among your strongest tools for success. Many people have been exposed to the idea of using affirmations to support dreams and goals, but few people learn how to harness their full potential. My intention is to share the value of using affirmations so that you can move confidently toward your highest inspirations.

## The Impact of Words

Words convey different meanings to different people and to the same person depending on the emotional state they are in. Therefore, to obtain the most impact when using affirmations, choose words that are clear and precise. Select words that resonate within you.

## Guidelines for Powerful Words:

The following guidelines will assist you in attaining the maximum benefit of affirmations.

➤ Choose words that apply to your current or future situation(s).

➤ Write your affirmations in a concise and simple way.

➤ Write words of power in the present tense.

➤ Avoid words such as "always," "never," and "not."

Throughout the ages, human beings have been using words to communicate with others. The ability to effectively verbalize our intent or desire empowers us and increases the likelihood that we will manifest the outcome that we're seeking. As an example, think of a lawyer defending his client in court trying to influence the jury's decision by using carefully selected words that can prove his client's innocence. The choice of words will definitely have an impact in the jury's minds and will likely influence their decision-making process.

Powerful words found in affirmations are purposefully used to communicate with yourself, and more precisely, with your mind. Thus, when choosing affirmations, be intentionally selective in regards to the wording in order to create the greatest impact. For example, there is a difference between saying, "I am good," and saying, "I am the best that I can be." It's better still if you say, "I am perfect." The latter, when repeated over a period of time, will leave a more powerful and meaningful imprint within your mind than the first two.

Powerful words release a current of life energy by increasing the frequency of nerve impulses inside the brain, which in turn change your brain's psycho-physiological pattern of habit.

Your mind will eventually influence your body's physiology and the actions that you take daily.

Words can have an uplifting effect by motivating and inspiring the person that repeats them frequently. This can negate or even overcome the break-down effect of the less desirable words that we are "bombarded" with daily from the media, co-workers, family members, friends, and ourselves. We've all seen, met, or heard of a person who as a child was constantly told by one or both of their parents, that they were stupid, or in some way inadequate. What that does over a period of time is set up a pattern within the mind, which believes it to be true. As an adult, this individual often has low self-esteem and poor self-confidence. Many of these people cycle through alternating stages of elation and depression because they don't believe in themselves.

Thus, powerful words and affirmations repeated consistently over a period of time can influence your whole being, doing, and having. Choose your words wisely!

# Purpose of Affirmations

Powerful words and affirmations help you get in tune with your purpose in life each time you say them. They also help you stay away from distractions and tangents that take you away from your purpose. The strongest affirmations are related to unconditional love, equilibrium, and wisdom. By repeating them several times a day, they shift your perceptions.

As this shift in perception takes place inside of you, events take on a new meaning and the dynamics surrounding you also change. You will begin attracting what you set out to be, do, and have. I suggest that you select or write at least one affirmation for every area of your life. You may have up to two or three for each area, however, more is not necessarily better. You want to be focused and specific. In order to do so, it is wise to be concise. By keeping it to one or a few affirmations for each area of life you will gain efficiency.

Different authors have arranged the areas of life in various groups and numbers. For example:

➤ Dr. Scott Walker, in his seminar N.E.T. SUCCESS, talks about nine areas of life. They are: Home, Ethics, Finance, Recreation, Education, Health, Career, Spiritual and Family. (For more information, contact N.E.T. Inc. at 800-888-4638)

➤ Dr. John F. Demartini, in his seminar Prophecy,™ identifies the following seven areas of life: Spiritual, Social, Family, Physical, Mental, Financial, and Vocational. (For more information, contact The Concourse of Wisdom at 888-DEMARTINI.)

If you choose to organize your affirmations by the seven areas of life, you can devote each day of the week to a specific area. By the end of the week you will have affirmed your goals in all areas and repeatedly stated all of your affirmations.

You may at any time include another affirmation from a different area in which you feel challenged, or that you hold as a high priority. Powerful words and affirmations are for the serious seeker of truth who is willing and disciplined to be consistent and persistent — no matter what. They are for those who are ready to repeat daily words that their superconscious mind will bring into the conscious mind to transform their reality.

# How to Use Affirmations

As you begin integrating powerful words and affirmations into your daily living, keep in mind that they will have a stronger impact upon your mind over time and with repetition. By stating your affirmations daily, they will empower you to attain your purpose in life.

1.  As you read the affirmations that you have chosen or written yourself, do so with intent. Say and repeat the affirmation in a state of sincerity and gratitude. In so doing, you open up the connection between the heart and the mind. Other variables are the pitch and tone of your voice while repeating the words out loud.

2.  Affirmations may be said silently, but by adding the dimension of sound, the impact to the mind is amplified. As you speak out loud, you are actually hearing the molecules of air vibrating your vocal cords.

    At a higher pitch, such as in a female voice, a word or note often registers at a higher frequency (vibration per seconds = Hertz = Hz) than that same word or note spoken by a man. You will create a stronger impact upon the brain by using your actual, pleasant pitch than trying to use a pitch that is higher or lower than your everyday speaking voice. However, if you're having a "low energy" day and you want to lift yourself up, you can consciously increase the pitch of your voice in order to resonate at a higher frequency and thus deliberately change the vibrational state of your whole being. As for the tone, keep the voice lively rather than monotonous. This tends to keep the brain function set and the mind awake.

3.  Recording your affirmations in your own voice is a wise way of obtaining the maximum benefit of affirmations. By hearing yourself saying the powerful words contained within each affirmation, your mind can quickly believe it is true. The sooner you believe it, the sooner it becomes so.

4.    As you experiment with repeating your words of power, pay attention to the sensation of resonance within you. Resonance is the connection of the words to you and your intent. It can be felt in various ways. Most of the time, it's a sensation of fullness, presence, appreciation, clarity and/ or empowerment. These may be felt individually, or all together. As long as you feel a link or bond between the affirmation and your reality, you will resonate with it and change your state of being and vibration. As you repeat powerful words in your everyday conversations and/or affirmations, you will fine-tune your resonance and attune to higher levels of energy.

Powerful words and affirmations can be found in various writings and in different forms of media (specialized magazines, books, and the Internet) or you can formulate your own.

Those you write yourself often leave a stronger imprint within the mind since they emerge from a thought (nervous system impulse) within your brain. Those that you collect from various sources will have the same effect as you repeat them over time and they become a part of you. It is best to handwrite your affirmations on index cards. By writing them down, you will make a greater impact on your mind. The strength of your affirmation is increased because you're using both the visual and the kinesthetic (touch) mode. Together, they encrypt your body, mind, and soul to attune your desired realities to your purpose in life.

Again, by keeping the total number of affirmations to seven or nine, you can change the affirmation card daily and repeat that affirmation as often as you want throughout the day. By changing the card each day, you create an easy system that will soon become a helpful habit.

You can add a new affirmation whenever you feel called to do so. You can also delete old words of power that no longer resonate with you. Allow your words of power to be flexible so that you can alter them according to your priorities and highest values.

# How to Formulate Your Own Affirmations

Formulating your own affirmations tends to create a quicker connection and imprint on your brain. However, if you are just beginning to use affirmations, using those "ready-made" by somebody else is fine, as long as they resonate with your realities and purpose in life.

As you integrate the process of daily affirmations into your life, new impulses/thoughts will emerge to help you come up with your own powerful words of inspiration and wisdom.

When formulating your own affirmations, in addition to being clear and precise, keep the length as short as possible. This will keep your mind focused on your purpose.

By using specific words and verbs (actions) such as do (doing), have (having) and be (being), you will poise yourself for taking action as opportunities present themselves. By being very specific in your affirmations you will immediately know if the opportunities correspond to your purpose. Thus, you can act upon the opportunity or let it go by without causing distraction in your present situation and evolution.

Be sure to link all of your affirmations to your primary purpose in life. By doing this, you will be inspired to repeat them daily for the rest of your life.

Words of power serve you in your communication with yourself. They also empower and inspire you to take actions. As you repeat your affirmations daily and refine the link to your purpose, you will continue to move steadily in the direction of your dreams.

# Powerful Words –
# A List of Affirmations

Each of the following affirmations corresponds with one of the seven areas of life. If they resonate with you, feel free to use them! You can also use them as examples for formulating your own.

- Spiritual: I am inspired daily.

- Mental: I am a master linker to my purpose.

- Physical: I am healthy. I am alive.

- Social: I love sharing with and teaching others what I learn and observe.

- Family: I thank myself for being who I am.

- Vocational: I am a master at asking quality and precise questions to empower my life and the lives of my clients.

- Financial: As I grow in self-worth so does my financial net worth.

The following are some of the words of power that have inspired me and many of my clients to pursue our goals and dreams. They are designed to inspire you on your quest to greater breakthroughs to success.

➤ I am an intelligent human being.

➤ I appreciate the fact that I am here to experience, evolve, and love.

➤ I am worthy of giving and receiving unconditional love.

➤ I love who I am and who I am becoming.

➤ I grow through challenges, support, and love.

➤ I am a master of my life and destiny.

➤ I accept becoming who I truly am.

➤ I am ready to evolve in the financial area of my life (any area of life).

➤ I create a master plan for my life and put it into action.

➤ I use my financial resources wisely.

➤ I am a whole and divine human being.

➤ I pursue my goals and take the steps to attain them.

➤ I feel gratitude and inspiration in regard to all past, present, and future experiences.

➤ By truly being who I am, others appreciate and respect me.

➤ I welcome challenges, for this is how I grow the most.

➤ Every day I pursue my goals to make them reality.

➤ What I like in others, I have in me. What I dislike in others, I have in me. Others are my mirrors for me to love and grow.

# The Truth About the Power of Words

1.  The use of powerful words and affirmations leaves a strong impact on the mind.

2.  Affirmations repeated daily empower and inspire you to action.

3.  The words in your affirmations should resonate with you, and be spoken in the proper pitch and tone of your voice.

4.  When formulating your own affirmations, be clear and precise, and link them to all seven areas of your life.

5.  When you record your affirmations on an audiocassette, and you listen to them, they create an even greater impact upon your mind and in your life by listening to your own voice.

# Begin Today!

The more you read about a subject the more knowledgeable you become about that subject. Therefore, I encourage you to read other essays and books on affirmations. As you do so, your understanding of the power in words will deepen and you will reap greater benefits from this inspiring practice. As your affirmations begin to manifest and you move closer to your dreams and goals, your appreciation for the profound impact of words will exponentially increase. The daily use of affirmations will empower and inspire you to break through to the success that you deserve. The day to begin is today!

\* \* \* \* \* \* \*

In Chapter Three, explore the empowering secrets of unlimited love.

# About Dr. Riccardo J. Cifola

D r. Riccardo J. Cifola is a chiropractor and consultant. He has been in private practice since 1987, and currently owns and operates Dr. Riccardo Cifola and Associates Chiropractic Office in Rosemère, Québec.

Throughout his quest for knowledge, Dr. Cifola has had the opportunity to study with such great minds as Dr. George Goodheart, who conceptualized Applied Kinesiology (A.K.); Dr. Jeffrey Bland, a pioneer in nutrition in preventive medicine; Dr. Scott Walker, founder of the Neuro-Emotional Technique (N.E.T.); Dr. Lawrence Newsum, founder and developer of the Bio-Kinetics Health System (B.K.); and Dr. John F. Demartini, founder of The Concourse of Wisdom School of Philosophy and Healing and author of *Count your Blessings: The Healing Power of Gratitude and Love.*

Dr. Cifola has recently released his Whole Health Seminar in an audiocassette format. The accompanying manual is the same text he uses in the live version of this workshop, which he offers across North America.

Dr. Cifola was born and raised in the Eastern Townships of the province of Québec by a French Canadian mother and an Italian father. He and his lovely wife, Lori, along with their two adorable daughters, Kayla and Pamela, live on the North Shore of Montreal.

# Dr. Riccardo Cifola & Associates

132, Boulevard Cure Labelle
Suite 105
Rosemère, Province of Québec J7A2H1

(450) 430-1555 or toll-free at (877) 708-1555
E-mail: DrRJCifola@AOL.com

Dr. Riccardo J. Cifola offers a simple, fast, and effective global health care approach. His mission is to guide his clients in regaining equilibrium in their health and personal lives. His clients come from all walks of life and consult with him for various reasons ranging from physical disorders to getting reconnected with their purpose in life. Half-day or full-day care is provided to those who require it and for those who come from out of town.

Dr. Cifola, whose recognition is continually expanding, loves to teach and share with his clients. When people gather around him and listen to what he has to say, they can feel his presence and appreciation for the opportunity of empowering others. Those ready to apply his teachings are bound to experience a transformation in their lives.

## Services:

➤ Biokinetic Chiropractic Health Care (www.biokineticshealth.com)

➤ Neuro-Emotional Technique (www.netmindbody.com)

➤ Nutritional Education and Personalized Plans

➤ Life Consulting and Coaching

# Seminars:

### Edifying Your Life

This one-day seminar will put you on purpose in all areas of your life. Participants learn how to design, plan, and implement the life of their dreams. (This seminar is soon to be released as an audiocassette program.)

For further information, to order a copy of
the Whole Health audiocassette program,
or to consult with Dr. Cifola, contact
Dr. Riccardo Cifola and Associates.

## CHAPTER·THREE

# You Can Not Lose
# the Ones You Love

*by*
*Mark A. Lorenson*

# You Can Not Lose the Ones You Love

### Mark A. Lorenson

---

*"In all ten directions of the universe, there is only one truth. When we see clearly, the great teachings are the same. What can ever be lost? What can be attained? If we attain something, it was there from the beginning of time. If we lose something, it is hiding somewhere near us."*

– Ryokan

---

I s it possible that love *really is* eternally present and can not be limited by time or space? If so, could we, during a moment of unconditional love, actually feel the loving presence of someone who is distant or deceased?

My research and experiences have convinced me that the answer to both questions is, "Yes!"

Yet, when a relationship ends or a loved one moves away or dies, many people experience a deep sense of loss. "Losing a loved one," can be one of life's most stressful and emotionally painful events. Ironically, the sadness and loneliness we feel perpetuates the perceptions of distance and separation. Gratitude and love can become blocked by feelings of loss, and holding onto these "hurts" can become a form of bondage.

In order to have the energy and focus to live our dreams, it is imperative that we learn how to balance our emotions and transform our illusions of "missing." In a universe that is actually "timeless" and "spaceless," how could anyone be missing? Where would they go? Our emotions may fool us, but our heart knows the truth. When we open our heart to unconditional and unbounded love, no one *can* be "missing." In these moments we learn, *by experience*, that love is always present and available to us.

I share this from the perspective of someone who has experienced his share of "missing" and "loss." My partner lives on the opposite side of the continent, my mother died when I was four, and my father took his own life when I was 24. My goal is to assist you to expand your current understanding, so that instead of missing the ones you love, you can open your heart to them and experience their loving presence.

## Who Do You Miss?

*"You were born together, and together you shall be forevermore...But let there be spaces in your togetherness, and let the winds of the heavens dance between you."*

– Kahlil Gibran

"I love you and I miss you." It's a phrase we hear almost daily through our movies and music. We've all heard countless variations of this story line: John feels "broken-hearted" because he's no longer with Mary. Life was "better" when Mary was "still around" and now that she's "no longer present" he misses her.

"We miss the ones we love" is a teaching and belief system so reinforced and widespread, that it's assumed to be true. I frequently encounter this "conventional wisdom" in my transformational consultations. I often work with people who, because of death, divorce, or some other kind of physical separation, "miss" the one they love. They think they miss their loved one, because that person is not physically present, just as I thought I missed my parents because they had died. But, I now know that we miss our loved ones because our sadness, anger, or loneliness closes our hearts to their ever-present love.

For example, when I was four years old and my brother, Jimmy, was one, Mom explained that she was going to the hospital to have an operation. She said she would be home in a few days.

But she didn't come home. A complication arose after the surgery and she died in the recovery room. I remember my father slumped in our living room chair with his head in his hands. It was the first time I ever saw him cry.

For months, each time the doorbell rang, I ran to the front door, calling, "Mommy, Mommy!" thinking and hoping that she was finally home. I was sad and I was angry. Since I was only a child, I didn't know that those emotions were keeping me from feeling my mother's love, which was there all along.

My mother's death was, in many ways, an awakening for me. Although I didn't know it then, I was learning that unconditional love is truly unlimited. For instance, there were times when I was daydreaming about Mom and feeling grateful, and suddenly it was as if she was sitting right next to me. I thought these moments of presence were random and unpredictable, but I've since learned that we can experience these moments any time we open our hearts.

# Creating a New Experience

*"Remorse, bereavement, and grief are nothing more than un-communicated appreciation and love."*

– Dr. John F. Demartini
*The Breakthrough Experience*™

What if we, through our current beliefs, are actually creating our experience of "missing?" Could shifting to a new understanding create a new experience? Could this new experience be a more heartfelt, profound, and deeper state of love where we no longer perceive the person to be "missing?" What would happen if we awakened to a new realization of "in moments of *unconditional* love, no one is, or can be, missing?" What if love just "loves" and we only "miss" when our hearts are *closed*? Would it then be possible for us to transform our grief into unconditional love, by expressing our gratitude to the ones we miss? Once you experience the presence of your "non-local" loved ones, you will more fully understand that the possibilities I have posed, are in fact, profound and liberating truths.

For me, the key to entering this new experience was to broaden my understanding from, "I love them and miss them" to "I love them and feel their presence." Intellectually, I understood that it's impossible to be separated from someone in space and time, during a "moment" of unconditional love that is spaceless and timeless. I also knew that the entire universe is holographic, so nothing and no one can ever truly be missing. In addition, I had read Dr. John F. Demartini, Larry Dossey, and other writers who taught on the principles of "non-locality" and I opened myself to the possibility of *experiencing* this "non-local love." When I was finally able to do this, my concept of love exponentially expanded. As a result, my overall experience of life is more meaningful and fulfilling.

Once I understood this powerful new philosophy and began applying it, I was able to create a new experience for myself — an experience where love equals *presence* rather than *missing*. This more expansive reality is based on The First Thermodynamic Law of Conservation, which states: "Nothing can be created or destroyed, it can only change in form." In a universe that conserves all energy, how could there be mortality?

What if whatever I love about the person I miss, is actually present in another form or forms? If so, my ability to identify these new forms, or "transformations," could create a new, more appreciative experience of life and love. In *this* experience, I could scan my life at any moment and realize that *every* aspect of anyone I miss is equally present in some form.

How liberating to realize that I can never truly lose what I love! When I discover the new form or forms of whatever I miss, I free myself from the distracting depression of loss and elation of gain. Identifying these transformations frees us and opens up an experience of life that's fulfilling, empowering, and appreciative. Overlooking life's transformations limits us and restricts us to an experience that's "lacking," disempowering, and unappreciative.

Years ago, when my father "passed-away" I had moments when I felt deep loss and grief. The perception that I "lost" my father was one way of looking at that event which created one kind of experience. Later, after opening myself up to a different way of looking at my father's death, I was able to create a different kind of experience.

It's this new and more profound experience that I would love to pass onto you. It is my hope that you, too, experience these moments of connection that are so heartfelt and fulfilling that they can only be described as beyond happy, sad, pleasure, pain, loss, or gain. It's in these illuminating moments of truth that you fully realize that you can not lose the ones you love.

For example, when I began to look at the experience that I had created around my father's death, the first question I asked was, "What, specifically, do I miss?" One by one, I listed the qualities that I "missed" about my father, such as his companionship, guidance, jokes, entrepreneurial spirit, etc.

Then, I began to look for his transformations. At the moment of his departure, who immediately became my close companion? Who began giving me their guidance? Who was the new joke teller? Where was the entrepreneurial spirit? One by one I located the transformations and found the new forms of Dad. I saw that some of his traits were concentrated in one person, while other aspects were dispersed among many. I even found that some of my father's traits had taken on a new life in me as my own entrepreneurial spirit awakened. Could it be that the essence of my father lived on in those around me and in me? The more transformations I recognized and identified, the more my experience began to shift from one of loss and sorrow to one of connection and gratitude.

As human beings, we live in a world of "form" and we can get attached to the form, sometimes even more so than the essence. When I'm working with clients, I often meet with initial resistance when I ask them to find the new forms that their "lost" loved ones have taken. They say things like, "But that's not the same as having all the traits together in the form of the one I love." One woman, whose father recently died, said, "I can see that his essence has changed form and I can even see who is expressing the traits that I miss about him, but I still miss my dad. Finding all the things I love about him in other people, just isn't the same."

To assist my clients in embracing the transformations, I ask them the same questions that I asked myself, when I was working through my father's death:

"What are the benefits of the new forms of Dad?"

"How is it serving my life *right now* to have Dad in these new forms?"

In my case, I found that many of the "lost" characteristics of Dad had suddenly shown up in the form of mentors at work. These mentors became close companions who were providing me with, not only "fatherly advice," but also career guidance and overall life wisdom. When I asked how that was serving my life, I realized that I had been given exactly what was needed to further my growth, life, and career, which incidentally was precisely what my father most wanted for me.

I also realized that much of the fatherly advice and guidance had shown up in the form of Wayne Dyer and other personal development authors through their books and tapes. It was exactly what was needed to lead me onto my path as a personal development and transformational consultant.

You might say we miss someone, not because they're "gone," but because we miss recognizing where and how they're still here. It was upon the moment of my father's death that a dream of mine was born. This dream was to understand the source of our emotions and use this knowledge to assist others in their growth and transformation. Through this event, I could see that there was no death without a birth. In my life, what was born was an entrepreneur who is dedicated to helping others transform their feelings of loss, and other bi-polar emotions, into gratitude and unconditional love.

How did my father's "death" serve my life? It gave me a mission. It put me on my path of purpose and allowed me to witness, firsthand, that those we love remain an integral part of our lives, whether they are near or far, alive or physically deceased.

Today, I find deep fulfillment in working with people who feel they have "loved and lost." It is incredibly rewarding to support and challenge these clients to take a deeper look. Upon a more thorough inspection, they unfold a new and more appreciative understanding. They awaken to the realization that no one is gone or missing; their loved one is present in ways they had not been recognizing. Helping people to transform their painful perceptions is one of the most inspiring aspects of my private practice because it opens them up to the experience of non-local, ever-present love. They realize, that what they were "missing" was there for them all along, but it was overlooked and unappreciated. The Grand Organizing Design of the universe, which conserves all energy, assures that nothing can ever be lost or missing.

## Who's "Missing?"

To free yourself from the illusions of "loss," take the following steps:

**Step #1** – Write the name of the person you are missing.

You can repeat this process as many times as you choose, but it is imperative that you work with only one person at a time.

**Step #2** – List all of the traits and attributes that you miss about this person.

The key is to be very specific. Is it the support, companionship, ability to listen, hugs, or smile, etc.? Reflect on and list exactly what you feel you have lost.

**Step #3** – Identify the transformations.

For each item on the list you made in Step #2, write down the answers for the questions below.

Who or what new form or forms have taken their (or its) place?

Who immediately showed up to give you support, companionship, the ability to listen, their hugs and their smile, etc.?

Keep in mind that you may find the transformations in the form of one person or many. Most importantly, keep looking until you recognize that every aspect of whomever you thought was missing is equally present in your life today.

# Out of Your Fantasy; Into Your Heart

*"When you understand how to love one thing,
then you also understand how to love everything."*

– Novalis

Your heart knows the truth of love, but human illusions can prevent you from experiencing love's power. Many people know that when they are grieving or missing someone, their heart is closed by these overwhelming emotions. However, few people realize that the extreme opposite of these emotions, such as elation and infatuation, keep the heart closed as well.

Often, when a client is having difficulty opening their heart to a "lost" loved one, or finding that loved one's transformations, it's because they're infatuated with this person and not embracing the totality of their loved one. Feelings of ingratitude — not only in the form of unresolved emotional resentments — but also in the form of unresolved infatuations, lock your heart and keep you from freely opening up and feeling the presence of those you love. Experiencing gratitude and *unconditional* love requires a perfectly balanced (positive and negative) perspective.

An example of this is the death of a celebrity. When our celebrities die, we focus mainly on their "good" and "positive" aspects. However, focusing only on the "positives," not only *raises our infatuation*, but simultaneously *deepens our depression* with "losing" them! Think about it. When society is *resentful* of someone they are "*glad* they're dead." Conversely, if they are *infatuated* with someone, they are "*sad* they're dead."

It's ironic. We think it's loving to *point out only his or her "good,"* when in actuality, this is the very thing that builds our infatuation and *blocks* our experience of appreciation and love for them.

I suggest a more balanced perspective. I propose that to *truly* appreciate and *unconditionally* love someone is to honor them in their entirety — acknowledging a perfect balance of their "positive" and "negative" traits, whether they're "alive" or "dead." This more balanced level of awareness helps us see how we block unconditional love with our praise and reprimand, infatuation and resentment, elation and depression, and other lopsided judgments and feelings. Bi-polar emotions reveal our imbalanced perceptions about people, events, or circumstances. When we balance our perceptions, we center ourselves in gratitude and unconditional love. When our hearts are open, the people we love are present.

## *Balancing Your Emotional Scales*

Take a moment, right now, and balance the infatuations and resentments that are preventing you from the experience of presence and love.

Divide a sheet of paper down the middle, from top to bottom.

On the top, left side of the paper, write the word "Benefits."
On the top, right side of the paper, write the word "Drawbacks."

### If infatuation is closing your heart:

Under the word, "Benefits," list all of the traits that you admire in your loved one. (Put only one trait on each line.)

Next to each trait you listed as a Benefit, write down all the ways this positive trait is a drawback to you and others. Continue finding drawbacks to this benefit, until your infatuation dissolves and you can see that this trait is equally positive and negative.

### If resentment is closing your heart:

Under the word, "Drawbacks," list all of the traits that you dislike or are angry about in your loved one. (Put only one trait on each line.)

Next to each trait you listed as a Drawback, write down all the ways this negative trait is a benefit to you and others. Continue finding benefits to this drawback, until your resentment dissolves and you can see that this trait is equally negative and positive.

Opening your heart to the totality of your loved ones awakens you to one of the most profound experiences in life — the experience of non-local, unconditional love.

For instance, I live in Ohio, and my significant other lives in Los Angeles. When our relationship comes up in conversation, we both typically hear the same line: "You must really miss each other." Our response? "Only when our hearts are closed."

We also hear a lot of "misbeliefs" about love. Often, people say, "Boy…long-distance relationships are tough." To which I respond, "What distance?" This response usually elicits flattened eyebrows, a tilted head, and a look of confusion.

My point is that two people sitting side by side, whose hearts are closed, can feel as if they're a thousand miles apart. Conversely, two people a thousand miles apart, whose hearts are open, can feel as if they're right next to one another. You can't commit to always being together physically, but you *can* commit to loving unconditionally.

Many confuse love with expectation. They *expect* a person to behave a certain way, and remain in a certain location. Learning to open your heart and love unconditionally and non-locally allows you experiences beyond the perceived limitations of typical relationships. When your heart is opened through balance and gratitude, you feel the presence of the one you love. It is in these life-changing moments of unconditional love that you'll know that wherever your dreams may lead, the ones you love will be with you always.

\* \* \* \* \* \* \*

In Chapter Four, learn how to break through polarity.

# About Mark A. Lorenson

**M**ark A. Lorenson is a professional speaker, consultant, and modern-day philosopher. He is the founder of Universal Consulting, a company devoted to personal development and human potential. He is also a co-author of *Breakthrough Secrets to Live Your Dreams*, the first book in the Breakthrough series.

Mark is certified to teach Transformation and The Breakthrough Experience™ Seminar through The Concourse of Wisdom School of Philosophy and Healing, based in Houston, Texas. His life is dedicated to the study and teaching of Universal Principles, metaphysics, and breakthroughs in human psychology. His seminars and books share the secrets of mastery that he has been learning and applying since his teens.

Mark is also the "Number One Rated" afternoon radio personality for WNCI Radio; one of the highest ranked FM stations in the nation. WNCI listeners know him as Chris Davis. Mark knows the meaning of grabbing one's vision and getting to work. He received his calling at a very young age and began taking action steps almost immediately.

Driven by his love of music and entertainment, he made his way onto the airwaves by the time he was a junior at Central High School in Salina, Kansas. During his senior year, he spent weekends working at two different radio stations — one a Contemporary Hit Radio Station (Top 40), the other Country. Mark quickly learned how to adapt his style for his vastly different shows, which ran back to back! Today, he uses this same talent to adapt his inspiring message to the wide array of individuals and organizations that seek his wisdom and knowledge.

Mark says, "Every one of us has the power to create an extraordinary life that's meaningful and deeply fulfilling. Masters of life are those who are awakened to and driven by the calling on the inside, more so than the people, and events on the outside. Perceptions of gain or loss, infatuation or resentment, joy or sorrow are bi-polar extremes that we create through our imbalanced perspective. When our perceptions are perfectly balanced we merge the two polarities and experience a momentary glimpse beyond the world of opposites. It is in these moments that we transcend loss and gain, pleasure and pain, and experience the transformational power of gratitude and unconditional love."

# Universal Consulting
## *Awakening Greater Life Mastery*

P.O. Box 566
New Albany, Ohio 43054

phone: 614-478-7814
www.UniversalConsult.com

Universal Consulting was founded for those desiring a purposeful life that's meaningful and deeply fulfilling.

Mark A. Lorenson specializes in a "full quantum" approach to personal and professional transformation. Uncover, resolve, and dissolve whatever issues, challenges, and obstacles you may be facing. Awaken your higher levels of love and gratitude and break through to a life filled with Vision, Inspiration, and Purpose!

## Services:

➤ Private, personal development coaching
(in person or by phone)
➤ Transformational consulting for individuals, the radio and entertainment industry, families, and organizations
➤ Speaking Engagements
➤ Customized workshops and seminars for individuals and groups
➤ The Quantum Collapse Process™

## Areas of Consulting Expertise:

➤ Conflict resolution
➤ Understanding and appreciating others
➤ Relationship building and "broken-heart" mending

➤ Increasing self-worth
➤ Distraction resolution
➤ Focusing in on your highest goals
➤ Grief and loss
➤ Turning stress into success
➤ Transforming charged emotions into love
➤ Unveiling purpose and increasing clarity of vision
➤ Aligning your team or staff with your inspired vision

# Seminars:

### Transformation

Experience a transformation in your life.

Discover the secret for turning any crisis into a blessing. Learn The Quantum Collapse Process™ a masterful tool for transforming charged emotions into love. Open your heart and experience more love for yourself and others. Awaken to the truth of how magnificent you really are!

# Books:

### *Breakthrough Secrets to Live Your Dreams*

North America's most dynamic authorities in personal and professional transformation reveal a treasure chest of tips, insights, strategies, and pearls of wisdom that will empower you to live your dreams.

### *Quotes for the Masters (Volumes I & II)— The Sages' Secrets for Greater Life Mastery*

Learn the secrets of the timeless sages. These books are packed with wisdom! Join the ranks of the masters by learning and applying their mind-expanding insights. Books of lessons from the masters for the masters. Priceless principles for anyone desiring greater life mastery!

# CHAPTER FOUR

# Key to Inner Kingdoms: Breaking Through Polarity

*by*
*Betty J. Pyykola*

# Key to Inner Kingdoms: Breaking Through Polarity

Betty J. Pyykola

---

*"The middle course is indeed the way of the highest virtue. But its practice has long been rare among the people."*

– Confucius

---

**M**y spiritual journey was a priority for about 10 years before I began to understand the power of the middle path. It happened in a transformational seminar when the presenter, Dr. John F. Demartini, asked for volunteers to share their most humbling experiences. I shared an event that took place when I was aspiring to be a nun.

As a punishment for accidentally dropping a hymnal over the choir balcony, I had to kneel on the hard terrazzo floor in the center of the chapel aisle for three hours a day for three months. All 240 aspiring nuns filed past me and took their seats to the right and left of me. They could only guess what debasing act I'd committed. As I related this story in The Breakthrough Experience™ seminar, I could still feel the resentment for my former Mother Superior.

In response to my story, Dr. Demartini said, "Your Mother Superior gave you a great gift. She put you right in the center revealing your great purpose — to stay on the middle path with the right and left in perfect equilibrium." The strong certainty in his voice echoed the truth in my heart.

The most valuable gift human beings have is the power to create their lives the way they would love them to be. Imagine you are the artist painting your life on the canvas of space and time. What do you want? An inspired masterpiece or a scene of quiet desperation?

If you chose a *masterpiece*, I have three fantastic tools that can unlock your powerful creative kingdoms. Each tool balances polarities and leads to a middle path. Balance is the key that opens the pathway to the inner realms of your mind and heart. This truth may seem novel, but it's not. It has been expressed in the art of ancient cultures for centuries. The sculpture of the Roman god, Janus, depicts the concept best. Janus holds the keys to higher realms. He is a two-faced god. One face looks left while an identical face looks right.

As you practice each tool, balancing right and left, positive and negative, you will reach a middle course where all levels of your mind are aligned with the inspiration of your soul. Once there, you can break through your physical, mental, and spiritual barriers to spheres of greater power and influence. The acronym KEY will help you remember the three tools that can assist you in reaching the middle path.

K    Keep a balanced breath with cellular commands.

E    Equilibrate the dual functions of the brain.

Y    Yield to the balance of lopsided perceptions.

# Breaking Through Physical Barriers

*"The foundation of all spiritual discipline consists
in the regulation of inspiration and expiration."*

– William James

## K – Keep a balanced breath with cellular commands.

Deep balanced breathing puts you into a trance-like state. In this state, you can command the cells, tissues, glands, and systems of your body. Dr. Ed Martin of the Path Foundation in Houston, Texas developed this method. I was initially skeptical, but when my colleague, Wanda, lost 90 pounds in 8 months, I could see that it was working.

Each morning and evening, Wanda practiced balanced breathing. When she reached the relaxed, creative realm of mind, she commanded the release of all causes of her excess weight and all blocks to having a healthy body. She then commanded her endocrine system, her digestive system, and her thyroid gland to return to their original imprint and coding. Wanda visualized her body as healthy and at its ideal weight. Not only did she improve her health and lose the extra weight, but she also saw shifts in other areas of her life.

To begin with, Wanda became inspired to be a certified hypnotherapist. As she worked with clients, she felt called to open her own business. Money started flowing in from unexpected sources. Soon, she was financially able to resign from her 20-year teaching career. Her husband was also able to resign. They achieved their life-long dream of working together in a broader sphere of influence helping children and adults heal in matters of body, mind, and soul.

Before using this tool, I strongly advise recording the following script in your own voice. Your inner mind loves listening to your own voice more than any other. Also you will stay in the deep-relaxed state with less difficulty. You can do this sitting up or lying down. For the best results, practice this method for 21 consecutive days.

### Balanced Breathing

To balance your breathing and enter a deep, relaxed state, follow the steps below.

1. Tilt your chin up 45 degrees (Omit if lying down).
2. Turn your eyes up toward the sky or ceiling.
3. Close your eyelids gently.
4. Inhale deeply for 6 counts (Stomach should be extending).
5. Hold for 3 counts.
6. Exhale for 6 counts (Stomach should be contracting).
7. Continue these counts for several minutes.

When you reach the deep, relaxed state, begin the cellular commands. (This is a shortened version of Dr. Martin's Cellular Command therapy. I have added the concept of divine perfection to this tool.)

### Cellular Commands

1. "Are there any (persons) you perceive as causing (name condition)" If the answer is no, ask about next cause.

2. "Are you willing to release these erroneous perceptions of these (people or conditions) and see the magnificent hidden order of these (people or situations) in your life?"

If the answer is no, say, "It does not serve your Soul's great purpose to hold onto these erroneous perceptions. Are you now willing?"

Usually the answer is yes. If the answer is no, this cause may best be handled by the third key later in this chapter.) Proceed with the next cause.

"I direct you, the subconscious mind, to release all false perceptions of (Dad's drinking) as causing my condition. Assist me in discovering the hidden order in my life."

3.  "If there is any reason that my conscious mind needs to know specifically of any perceived cause, I direct you, the subconscious mind to provide this information to my conscious mind in a loving manner."

4.  After all causes have been released, give the command to the part of the body that needs healing. It is wise to include the endocrine and immune systems. Direct each system and part of the body separately.

"I am willing to see this condition as a gift from the creator of my body. My body is teaching me what I have not yet learned to love. I am willing to acknowledge the divine perfection in any people, places, things, events, or ideas that I perceived as causing this condition."

Ask the subconscious about causes (Step 1). Proceed with Steps 2-4 immediately after each cause. Then go back and ask about the next cause. The causes you will inquire about are: persons, places, things, events, and ideas.

# Why Does This Method Work?

Balanced breathing enables the positive and negative ions in the air you breathe to become perfectly balanced in the channels of your nervous system. Negative ions enter your body through the left nostril and flow through the Ida channel on the left side of your spinal cord. Positive ions enter the right nostril and flow through the Pingula channel on the right side of your spinal cord. When your inhalations and exhalations are perfectly balanced, the sashimi nerve in the *center* of the spinal cord becomes active.

When the sashimi nerve is active, *both* the Ida and Pingula nerves open and the positive and negative ions fuse in the center creating a surge of energy rising up the spinal cord. The fusion of the polarized ions in the center channel calms the conscious mind so that the subconscious mind and all levels of the mind are in alignment with our Souls.

This inner realm of higher energy has command over the lower levels of mind that run your body. The commands communicate with the intelligence of each cell. Each cell is capable of returning to its original perfect DNA blueprint or coding through these commands once the causes have been released.

# Breaking Through Mental Barriers

*"Do you want to know the great drama of my life?
It's that I put my genius into my life."*

– Oscar Wilde

## E - Equilibrate the functions of your brain.

This tool awakens the genius in you. It takes you to the alpha/theta level of mind — a level where Einstein reportedly spent 90 percent of his time. You can enter the alpha/theta realm by causing your brain waves to cycle at a midpoint range, 7-14 cycles per second. Our conscious mind cycles around 15-20 cycles per second and while asleep usually 5 to 1 cycles per second. Notice how alpha/theta is the middle path.

When your brain cycles from the midpoint range, the information from your right hemisphere merges in the center with the information from your left hemisphere. The functions of the right and left hemispheres are equal but opposite. Most people allow the functions of the left brain to dominate over the functions of the right brain. The genius knows how to balance the functions — integrating sequential, logical information with creative, intuitive information. When this merging occurs, inspired ideas and solutions to problems are birthed.

Applying this tool is simple. You start with balanced breathing. Balanced breathing automatically takes you to the alpha/theta state. While in this state, you program your mind to perform desired functions by responding to certain signals. In this way, whenever you need the brain to perform these functions while in the conscious state, visualizing and mentally naming the three symbols will automatically cause the brain to perform the desired function.

You can use any symbols you like — letters, numbers, objects, shapes, etc. I use a circle, triangle, and cross because they are ancient archetypal symbols with special meaning. The circle symbolizes the All Knowing One. I think of myself as tapping into universal intelligence. The triangle is symbolic of the womb from which sprang all of creation. I think of entering the creative process. The cross symbolizes the joining of heaven and earth; matter and spirit. I think of my mind as aligned with the inspiration of my soul. Think of three symbols that attract you and complete the following steps:

1. Do balanced breathing as described in **K.**

2. Breathe deeply and on the exhale visualize and mentally say circle (or your own selected symbol) three times.

3. Breathe deeply and on the exhale visualize and say triangle (or your own selected symbol) three times.

4. Breathe deeply and on the exhale say cross (or your selected symbol) three times.

5. Give the specific commands you desire.

   For example:

   ➤ My concentration is perfectly focused when reading, studying, and listening to lectures.

   ➤ Everything I am learning is stored perfectly for easy recall.

   ➤ My mind easily organizes, comprehends, and integrates information.

   ➤ My mind can focus on detail and comprehend the whole picture simultaneously.

   ➤ Everything I am learning is easily accessible to me when I need it for writing, developing presentations, tests, etc. I continuously gain more confidence in myself as these abilities sharpen.

6. Awaken by counting yourself up from 1 to 5.

   Dr. Ed. Martin developed this tool, called Super Learning. Before using this tool, a trainer for a childcare agency struggled for three years with putting a series of six two-hour presentations together. She had a huge bookcase lined with books and materials on the topic. Each time she sat down to outline the concepts and organize the information, she felt overwhelmed. She could not figure out how to logically present the content in a way that would inspire participants to action.

Then she started using Super Learning. She started receiving stories, poems, and articles from others that served as a springboard to her presentation. She leafed through her volumes of material and could see exactly how the information could be congruently organized. Within two weeks she outlined and organized the material for all six lectures. Staff was deeply moved during her presentations. Everyone started working as a team to set goals and outline action steps. They were inspired to create the highest quality program in the childcare field.

# Breaking Through Spiritual Barriers

*"The world is not to be put into order;*
*the world is order — incarnate. It is for us*
*to harmonize with this order."*

– Henry Miller

## Y – Yield to unconditional love.

Most people agree that unconditional love is a very powerful state of being, but few people know how to actively open up to this level of love. However, when you balance your lopsided perceptions, and see the existing perfection, you experience a beautiful kingdom of love and gratitude.

One of the best tools I have learned to balance perceptions is The Quantum Collapse Process,™ created by Dr. John F. Demartini, founder of The Concourse of Wisdom School of Philosophy and Healing. The process is based on the laws of balance and is best learned in The Breakthrough Experience™

seminar. During this process, the *energy* spent in resentments or infatuations, fear or guilt about any person, place, thing, event, or idea transforms into pure unconditional love. One of the most revealing aspects of this process is finding the balance of positive and negative. When you discover the balance, you enter the kingdom.

For example, a couple of years ago, a very serious licensing violation occurred in my foster care program. Although I had not committed the violation, as director of the program I was ultimately responsible. This violation could have seriously affected our operation and licensure. The state was sending their ace agent to investigate. As I talked with her to set the date for the investigation, I heard the stern, rigid judgment in her voice. Fear, anger, and guilt gripped my whole being. As I started the equilibrating Quantum Collapse Process,™ something told me to focus on my mother. I didn't see how my mother, who lived a thousand miles away, had anything to do with present circumstances, but I followed that inner guidance.

I looked closely at my mother's traits that I perceived as negative. I found and listed the benefits of her judgment and the punishments that she had given me as I was growing up. I saw how all of the things that I didn't like about her actually served me in my growth and spiritual evolution. As I neared the end of this process, I felt an overwhelming gratitude for my mother. My heart opened to embrace her. As I looked up from my paper, I saw my mother's eyes filled with wisdom and love. And then I saw the eyes of each of my Mother Superiors in the very same way — each one coming into balance in a domino effect. I cannot adequately describe the love and lightness I felt.

I realized that the tremendous fear of being judged or punished during the upcoming investigation had disappeared. I knew I could relate to all the persons involved with an objectivity I had not possessed before. I knew that, whatever the outcome, the benefits and drawbacks balanced. These thoughts dominated my mind throughout the course of the investigation.

As it ended, the licensing agent turned to me and said, "I have closed many programs down. This is not one of them. This is a program that cares about children."

The Quantum Collapse Process™ takes us to a timeless, spaceless kingdom of love because it balances the polarity in our minds and opens our heart to the truth. The truth is there is always a balance of human traits in every person. There are equal benefits and drawbacks, support and challenge, pain and pleasure in everyone and everything. When we truly see this balance, we break through the tension of our polarity. The energy used to hold this tension transforms and takes us to the center of our inner being where there is only love.

If there is something in your life that represents the hard terrazzo beneath your knees, I encourage you to take a deeper look. I promise you that whatever it is, it's a gift for you, just as my experience was a gift for me. You now have the tools to assist you in breaking through the barriers in your life — physically, mentally, and spiritually. These keys take you to the middle path, unlocking the kingdoms of power within to create your life the way you would love it to be.

\* \* \* \* \* \* \*

In Chapter Five, learn how to put your fears aside and go!

# About Betty J. Pyykola

**B**etty Pyykola has devoted 35 years of her professional life to helping individuals, children, and parents experience better communication and loving relationships. Through her work as a trainer and consultant, she inspires people to find the hidden magnificence in the circumstances of their lives. Children and parents come to understand the role they play as teachers of love for each other and themselves.

Betty is a wife, mother, grandmother, mother-in-law, former foster parent and administrator of a therapeutic foster care and adoption program. She has an in-depth understanding of the physical, emotional, mental, and spiritual barriers that often hold members of a family in deep resentful ties that affect all areas of their lives. Betty's consulting, hypnotherapy, workshops, and seminars assist individuals, children, and families to achieve profound changes in thinking and behavior.

Betty is the founder of Star Journeys, a company dedicated to personal development for individuals, children, and families through the study, teaching, and application of universal principles. She received her undergraduate degree from Alveno College in Milwaukee, Wisconsin and her Master's Degree in Human Development and Family Living from the University of Kansas.

She is a certified child care administrator, an advanced certified clinical hypnotherapist specializing in Basic and Advanced Cell Command for physical conditions, addictions, grief, depression, post traumatic stress, and specialized hypnosis for children. Betty is also a certified facilitator of The Breakthrough Experience™ seminar and The Quantum Collapse Process™.

# Star Journeys

Betty J. Pyykola
9219 Pecos St.
Houston, TX 77055
email: starjourn@prodigy.net
phone: 713-464-9286.

Star Journeys is dedicated to personal development for individuals, children, and families through the study, teaching, and application of universal principles. We offer:

➤ Individual hypnotherapy for physical conditions, addictions, grief, depression, post traumatic stress and specialized hypnosis for children.

➤ Transformational consulting for individuals, families, children, and small groups.

➤ Full-day consultations using hypnotherapy and The Quantum Collapse Process.™

➤ Custom-designed motivational seminars for organizations.

## Seminars:

### Transformation

This full-day seminar will help you transcend any relationship you have with a person, place, thing, event or idea that is holding you back or pushing your buttons. Universal principles and The Quantum Collapse Process™ are taught and applied freeing you to live a more powerful and loving life.

## The Breakthrough Experience™

This two-day seminar is life changing. You will learn The Quantum Collapse Process™ that helps you transcend any issue or relationship that keeps you stuck. You will learn how to work with Universal principles to manifest what you would love to be, do, and have in all seven areas of life. This seminar can be tailored to special groups such as those experiencing grief and loss, foster parents, adoptive parents, adult children of alcoholics, etc.

## Children's Breakthrough

This seminar is the most profound seminar a child will ever attend. They will glimpse their true potential and focus on their purpose in life. They will learn Universal principles and how to apply them to have the life they would love to live. They will learn that no matter what someone has done or not done, including themselves, they are worthy of love. What greater gift can a child receive than to know how to love and be loved. This seminar is tailored for ages 8-12 years of age and 13-16 years of age.

For more information, or to schedule a one or two-day seminar in your city, contact Star Journeys.

# CHAPTER FIVE

# Put Your Fears Aside and Go!

*by*
*Patrick Snow*

# Put Your Fears Aside and Go!

Patrick Snow

---

*"Once a man has made a commitment to a way of life, he puts the greatest strength in the world behind him. It's something we call heart power. Once a man has made this commitment, nothing can stop him short of success."*

– Vince Lombardi

---

Like most people interested in reaching their dreams, you probably have given a great deal of thought to what you want to achieve, do, or become. I hope you've created written goals. You may also have developed additional materials, such as a plan or mission statement. All of these are important for success. Now is the time to begin implementing your plan and *go*! In other words, let's let the fun begin!

While this can be a very exciting time, this is also the point where many people falter. Why? Once the daydreaming, planning, and preparing are behind you; action must be taken. But to take action can be scary. When people have fears that are very strong, their actions are often ineffective—if they take any action at all.

Author David Joseph Schwartz, said, "Do what you fear and the fear disappears." This may be true, but taking that initial action can be difficult. I use several powerful statements to help me remember the importance of taking action:

**Action = Results**
**This year's efforts pay next year's bills.**
**Today's work will fund tomorrow's biggest dreams.**

The thoughts above are critical to overcoming inaction. Only by working *today* will you reap your dreams for *tomorrow*. Motivational speaker and author Les Brown said:

> *"You are currently molding your future;*
> *whatever you are now doing will result in*
> *what your future holds for you."*

Here's another way to look at the concept of taking action. I have saved the following excerpt from Murray McBride's forum for many years because I believe it emphasizes how important taking action is, especially when put in the context of fear:

> "Every morning in Africa, a gazelle wakes up. It knows it must out-run the fastest lion or it will be killed. Every morning in Africa, a lion wakes up. It knows it must out-run the slowest gazelle or it will starve. It doesn't matter whether you're a lion or a gazelle: *when the sun comes up, you'd better be running!*"

## *Exercise*

Think back to a time when you were ready to begin a big project, such as creating an important business report, applying for a new job, selling your house to buy a new one, or considering marriage or another long-term commitment.

Did fear arise?

_____

_____

How so?

_____

_____

What did you do to lessen and eventually overcome this fear?

_____

_____

What lessons about fear did this experience teach you?

_____

_____

# Everyone Has Fear

One of the main things to remember when fear arises within you is this: everyone has fears! The key is to accept this fact and *move forward despite your fears*. This, I believe, is the true meaning of courage!

Want an example? I don't think anyone in modern history has put their fear aside and gone out on a limb more than the late Dr. Martin Luther King. Dr. King concluded his last speech on April 3, 1963, in Memphis, Tennessee, with these words:

> *"Well, I don't know what will happen now; we've got some difficult times ahead. But it doesn't really matter with me now, because I have seen the mountaintop. And I don't mind. Like anybody, I would like to live a long life—longevity has its place. But I am not concerned about that now. I just want to do God's will. And He's allowed me to go up to the mountain. And I've looked over, and I've seen the Promised Land. And so I'm happy tonight: I'm not worried about anything; I'm fearing no man. Mine eyes have seen the glory of the coming of the Lord!"*

We all know the tragic fate of Dr. King. What's important to remember is that he put his fear aside and did what his heart told him to do. And because of that, he is arguably one of the most important world leaders to have ever lived. His human-rights accomplishments reverberated around the globe!

## *Exercise*

Take a moment to think about the dreams or activities that you have thought about doing, but have never done because of fear or apprehension. Make a list of these below.

_____

_____

_____

_____

Once you have completed your list, circle the ones you still have time to accomplish.

# You Must Cross the Bridge

Here's another way to think of addressing and overcoming fear when pursuing your life dreams and goals. The song, "Me," on the CD, *This Fire*, by Paula Cole, carries an empowering message of inspiration regarding fear. An excerpt from the lyrics says it all.

*"I am walking on the bridge,*
*I am over the water,*
*and I am scared as hell,*
*but I know there's something better,*
*yes—I know there's something better."*

What I believe she means is that we know there is something better *on the other side of the bridge*. Otherwise, why would our heart and soul send us across this bridge of fear? Your heart knows what is best for you, so listen to this calling and move on pursuing these dreams — despite your fears. It's okay to be afraid, *as long as you make certain that your fear doesn't stop you!*

I challenge you to listen to your heart, put your fears aside, and GO!

# How to Put Your Fears Aside

To succeed in life and reach your destiny, you must develop *belief* and *trust* in yourself. Author Anatole France said, "To accomplish great things we must not only act, but also dream; not only plan, but also believe."

Only when you trust your abilities and believe in yourself, can you overcome your fears and leap into whatever your heart is calling you to do. Here's a poem from an unknown author that represents this point well:

> *The jump is so frightening*
> *Between where I am,*
> *and where I want to be...*
> *Because of all I may become,*
> *I will close my eyes and leap!*

I know, I know—trusting yourself is easier said than done! Just like Dr. King, however, you must learn trust to put your fears aside and pursue your dreams.

## Fear Destruction Process

➤ You must make every moment count, because I believe that you only live on Earth *one time*.

➤ Study the true risk of the situation at hand. How much fear is legitimate, and how much is simply a manner of your own mind?

➤ Ask yourself, "If I don't do this, will it haunt me for the rest of my life?" Regret can be one of the most disappointing and disheartening human emotions!

➤ Ask yourself if something that you fear must be overcome to reach your goals. Focusing on what you can obtain, such as goals, helps reduce fear.

➤ Ask yourself, "Could the task at hand kill me?" I know this sounds extreme, but it also helps put things in perspective.

Overcoming fear and breaking through barriers are two of the most empowering things we can do. It is this belief that gave me the courage to face and overcome many of my own fears.

For example, each year my family vacations at Kaanapali Beach in Maui. There's a huge cliff formation that protrudes out into the ocean about a quarter of a mile. The cliff is called "Black Rock" and many of the local kids jump or dive off this 50-foot cliff for fun. After watching this for several days, my son, Sam, who was nine at the time, decided that he and his father were going to jump off this cliff into the ocean below. Later that day my wife overheard Sam telling some other kids what we were going to do. Well, to say the least, I hate jumping from high places, regardless of how deep the water is! Therefore, I soon found myself evaluating this challenge from every angle. Here's what came to me:

➤ I believe that I only live once, and I was, after all, on vacation.

➤ I studied the level of risk involved. I had seen many kids jump off that cliff, and no one had hit any rocks below. I even watched them enter the water from below the surface with my snorkel mask on.

➤ I then asked myself, "If I don't do this, what will my son think of me?" I wanted him to view me as a hero, just as I view my own Dad (a golfer, who has made a hole-in-one three times!).

➤ If I am to be adventurous, as one of my life goals indicates, then I should jump.

➤ Finally, I concluded that if I jumped out as far as I could, I would certainly miss the side of the cliff and land in the water. (I may hit the water awfully hard, but I knew I would *live!*)

With this due diligence behind me, my son and I both jumped off Black Rock. In fact, we did it twice! Let me tell you, it was quite a rush! My wife took pictures of both of us in mid-air and they turned out great! My son thinks I am a "hero" for jumping, and we will share this memory together forever!

Of course, not everyone has a taste for cliff-jumping adventures, so here's a career-related example about overcoming fear. I spent four years going back and forth as to whether or not I should hunker down and finish my book, *Creating Your Own Destiny*. I finally realized that the "true risk" to my career was to *not* follow through with what my heart had told me to do. My book and my speaking career are my passions, and I knew that if I was going to be truly fulfilled in life, I *must* act on these inspirations. If I hadn't listened to this internal message, three things could have happened:

➤ I could have spent the rest of my days regretting my lack of action and being disappointed in myself for not living up to my full potential.

➤ I could have been stuck in the idea that I had to work only in sales, rather than devoting my energy to sales as well as my other passions.

➤ I'd have been building wealth for someone else instead of for myself. I would probably also be questioning why I had limited my options to just "a job," when I could accomplish so much more.

If your heart is telling you what your passion is, then follow it and great things will happen in your life; I'm confident of this!

# Pain and Pleasure

Putting your fears aside can feel like a painful experience; I'll be the first to admit this because I've known my share of pain! But pain can be a positive. Before I explain how, here's a quick story: A mailman delivered the mail to an old man who sat on his porch with his dog. Every day the mailman would wonder why the dog was moaning. Finally the mailman asked the old man this question, and the old man replied, "There's a nail sticking up from the porch that's jabbing him in the side."

The mailman said, "Well then, why doesn't your dog get up and move?"

"Well, I guess it doesn't hurt enough to make him move," the old man replied.

Many pains are like the one being faced by the dog: pains that are small and nagging but not strong enough to motivate us. Well-known speaker and motivational coach Anthony Robbins says that human motivations (actions) stem from two main sources: our desire to avoid pain or our desire to gain pleasure.

If you have something jabbing you in the side of life, don't be afraid, like the old dog, and simply sit there and keep moaning. I challenge you to get up and do something about your pain. Take the necessary action steps to control your circumstances. I guarantee that if you do, you will be one step closer to creating your own destiny!

Putting your fears aside and *going* is challenging; I'm not going to say it isn't. Think, for example, of all that I went through before I jumped off that cliff! Now think of the cliffs in your life that are keeping you from achieving your goals. Ask yourself, "What cliffs do I need to jump off to move forward in life and become the type of person that I want to be?"

Eliminating or greatly reducing fear must take place for you to continue to move forward in the pursuit of your goals and your destiny. Review my *Fear Destruction Process* whenever you feel "frozen" with fear.

\* \* \* \* \* \*

In Chapter Six, discover the secrets to a fulfilling parent/ child relationship.

# About Patrick Snow

For almost 20 years, Patrick Snow has studied the field of personal growth and development. Today, as a motivational speaker, success coach, sales trainer, and author, he is an expert on how to discover and create your ultimate destiny in life. Patrick's book, *Creating Your Own Destiny*, was published in 2001, by Aviva Publishing, Lake Placid, NY.

Originally from Michigan, Patrick graduated from the University of Montana in 1991 with a degree in Political Science and a minor in Asian Studies. While attending college at U of M, he also studied Business Management and the Japanese Language. Upon graduation, he moved to Seattle, Washington, and has held various sales management positions at Fortune 500 companies, including Airborne Express and Avis. He has also spent several years in high-tech sales. Because of his income diversity philosophy, in addition to his speaking career, he has been selling printed circuit boards throughout the Pacific Northwest and Western Canada since 1996.

Patrick and his wife, Cheryl, a Criminal Deputy Prosecuting Attorney for King County in Seattle, have lived in the Puget Sound region since 1991. They have been blessed with two young boys, Samuel and Jacob. In addition to his busy career and family life, Patrick also volunteers his time in the community by teaching Japanese at a local elementary school and by coaching youth basketball and baseball.

# Patrick Snow

**The Snow Group**
Box 10864, Bainbridge Island, WA 98110
(800) 951-7721
Patrick@CreateYourOwnDestiny.com
www.CreateYourOwnDestiny.com

## The Book:

### *Creating Your Own Destiny*
**How to Get Exactly
What <u>You</u> Want
Out of Life**

## Patrick speaks on, and coaches *how to*:

➤ Visualize Your Dreams
➤ Set and Prioritize Your Goals
➤ Create Your Game Plan
➤ Build Wealth
➤ Know for Whom You Work
➤ Conquer Addictions and Overcome Adversity
➤ Put Your Fears Aside and GO!
➤ Remember Those Who Molded You
➤ Execute Your Plan Daily
➤ Develop Your Higher Calling

To receive your copy of *Creating Your Own Destiny*,
to book Patrick for a speaking engagement, or to
hire him as a success coach, please contact
The Snow Group.

# CHAPTER SIX

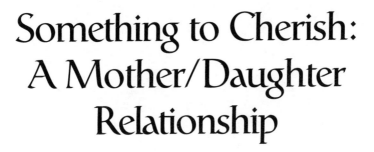

# Something to Cherish: A Mother/Daughter Relationship

*by*
*Susan A. Friedmann, CSP*
*&*
*Yael Friedmann*

# Something to Cherish: A Mother/Daughter Relationship

Susan A. Friedmann, CSP
&
Yael Friedmann

---

*"Honesty is the first chapter
in the book of wisdom."*

– Thomas Jefferson

---

## The Mother's View

**M**y daughter, Yael, and I recognized years ago that we had a special relationship, although, for a while I thought it completely normal. It was only when both her friends and mine commented about our intimate, honest conversations and ability to disclose our thoughts, dreams, likes, and dislikes, that I realized we shared something extraordinary.

I believe the true essence of our relationship lies in the honesty and respect we have for one another — something we continuously strive to expand. It is these two aspects that form the focal points of our chapter. We decided to write this together so that you can experience both sides of our relationship and share some of the magic that exists between us.

As the mother, I feel entitled to go first. My section of this chapter focuses on HONESTY. I use this word as an acronym to guide you through the seven steps that make our relationship succeed. My hope is that you gain insights that will help you discover some golden opportunities with your children.

## Have the guts to share your faults

Children tend to put parents on a pedestal and want to believe they can do no wrong. Yael was no different. Realizing I was far from perfect, this was a myth I wanted to quash as early as possible. I took every opportunity that presented itself to share my imperfections. I would, and still do, weave them into our conversations (and make them sound so natural.) I must admit that at first it was pretty tough to do. But the more I do it, the more I build a different reality — one much more in line with the true me. As Kahlil Gibran said, "Knowledge of the self is the mother of all knowledge."

## Own up and apologize

Another challenge is knowing when and how to apologize. As I mull over my past, I remember with remorse a person who frequently lapsed into fits of screaming, shouting, and threatening as a problem-solving mechanism. Growing up, I was exposed to the scream and shout method of dealing with issues, so it was no surprise that I continued this approach with my own family. Did it work? I suppose momentarily, but the long-term effects proved damaging. Both my son and daughter walked on eggshells around me just in case I unexpectedly flared up into a rage. It was usually the squabbling and sibling rivalry that ignited the fiery flame and set me off on my rampage. I know that when I'm out of balance, which often means stressed out, a simple apology goes a long way.

# Negate the past

Kids, like most of us, tend to do things that don't always resonate with a positive tone. Smoking, drinking, staying out past curfew, the list is endless. My husband, Alec, and I had two ways of dealing out reprimands depending on the severity of the misconduct, either we would choose or we would let the kids decide their own fate. Either way, it was important that no matter what the wrongdoing, we let bygones be bygones, and not dwell on the past error. Once it was over, it was ended.

This wasn't always the case. I used to criticize, dredge up previous difficulties, and blame others for everything that went wrong. I had a hard time letting things go. But, over the past 15 years I have done a tremendous amount of personal growth work through books, tapes, and seminars. This process has helped me to realize that letting go of the past is an essential ingredient for improving relationships.

# Express your feelings

Communicating and expressing feelings is one of the many lessons Yael has taught me, and it's one of the strong points in our relationship. She is a very caring, sensitive, and expressive young lady. Even growing up she wanted to share how she felt about one thing or another. I, on the other hand, experienced deep feelings but had a hard time actually vocalizing them. This was, and still is, one of Yael's real strengths. She has a knack for articulating her thoughts verbally, in writing, and in her artwork.

Do we have difficult times? Most definitely! We handle challenging situations by discussing them with total honesty using "I feel" statements. We know that sweeping issues under the rug or staying silent only delays the inevitable. Unspoken emotions tend to fester and develop into hideous monsters. I share my views in a logical way and when we don't see eye to eye, we might agree to disagree. We talk, we cry, we hug.

## Show respect

One of my strengths is that I continually show Yael respect for whatever she does. I may not always approve, but I allow her to express and be her own person. I try hard not to nag and once I've shared my feelings about a situation, I let it be. I don't expect to know everything about her life. I know she will disclose whatever she wants or needs to share. I try not to interfere and let her make her own decisions, although, on occasion, I offer what I consider as helpful hints.

There are times when she, like all of us, needs her private space to be alone. Over the years during stressful and challenging times, especially throughout those teenage years, she took solace in her diary, or in her art. I encouraged and supported her, listened, and gave her self-confidence at times when she thought her world was collapsing around her. At times like these, loving hugs help give her strength to face her dragons.

Having grown up in England with a very different upbringing and education, there are instances where I have a tough time understanding Yael's experiences. However, we truly value each other's differences. In the words of author, Maya Angelou, "If you find it in your heart to care for somebody else, you will have succeeded."

## Take time for unconditional love

I love Yael no matter what. Being a true Gemini, she has two sides. There is the loving, sensitive, caring side, and then there's the self-centered, cold "leave me alone" side. As much as I don't care for the latter side, I know it's all part of the whole of who she is, and I love her unconditionally. Whether or not I approve of things she does, she knows that I love her.

Since we live several states away from each other, speaking on the phone is an almost daily routine, sometimes even several times a day, depending on our needs. We both take time to stop whatever we're doing to spend a few minutes catching up, sharing, laughing, or crying. It's part of the unconditional love we have for each other and an important part of nurturing our connection.

## Yield to humor

Alec, my husband, Dov, my son, and Yael, have all taught and continue to teach me how to laugh at situations, life, and most of all, myself. We love to laugh together. Life is too short to be taken too seriously.

Mothers and daughters are individuals, not clones. I believe there's magic between two people when you show respect and are truly honest with each other. Growing up, I missed out on a really close mother/daughter relationship. As I cherish my relationship with Yael, so do I value my relationship with my own mother and feel that closeness and caring come with age and maturity. In the words of William Shakespeare, "No legacy is so rich as honesty."

# The Daughter's View

For years I took my relationship with my mother for granted. It was a challenge to write this chapter and analyze something which seems so basic and natural. However, as I thought back on the many occasions friends have been floored by what I said so casually in front of my parents, not for shock value, but simply because I was comfortable enough to be who I am, I realized there is a lot I can share.

My mother and I have a multifaceted relationship. She's my mother, but she's also my sounding board, confidant, and best friend. Honesty and respect are the pillars of our relationship This is what R-E-S-P-E-C-T means to me.

## Ritual togetherness

Mothers and daughters have their own lives. They are their own people, but they share a bond unlike any other. Finding time to spend together whether it's movie night, lunch, or curling up on the bed reading or talking, is an integral part of our relationship.

I used to get so jealous of my dad and my brother taking father-son trips together. They would go camping and I would feel left out. I longed for that kind of attention and so I approached my mom and asked for a trip together. She agreed and we've been taking time out to do special things together ever since.

One of my favorite memories is from a concert Mom and I went to when I was in high school. My brother bought me tickets for the Grateful Dead concert and then couldn't make it home to go with me. I couldn't drive yet and was having a hard time figuring out how I was going to travel an hour and a half to see the show. I dressed my mom up in jeans and a tie-dye T-shirt and dragged her to a concert and a scene she was completely unfamiliar with. I watched as she tried to blend in and dance on the lawn surrounded by hippies. It was a cultural experience for her and a wonderful bonding experience for us. We haven't repeated that experience but we've had others each with their own flavor.

*Make time to share.*

## Encourage each other

My mom has always been my biggest cheerleader. Not that she agrees with everything that I do, but she rarely stands in my way, unless she is scared for my safety. I have to add that when those times come up I take notice, since it is not the normal reaction.

The more I see my mother as a human being and a friend, the more I realize that I can support her too. She has undergone many challenges in her life and I am happy to be able to return the support she's given to me. For her fiftieth birthday, my brother and I split the cost of flying lessons for her. She once mentioned to me that she always wanted to learn to fly. I believe you're never too old to learn something new, so despite my dad's doubts, we signed her up for lessons. I think it's so cool that my mom had the courage to try something so thrill-seeking as flying a plane!

*Remember you're her biggest fan, just as much as she is yours.*

## Surrender control

This is a challenge for both of us, as we are both somewhat control freaks (I had to get it from somewhere). Neither of us knows what is best for the other, but if I hear her out, I know where she's coming from, even if I disagree. It doesn't always have to be my way or her way; many compromises have been reached over the years.

Sometimes my mom even goes so far as to tell me she can't deal with me and that she's had enough of hearing about something that I'm having a hard time with. Sure it hurts, but I appreciate her honesty. Her bluntness also gives me perspective because it shows me how much I've been carrying on about one thing or another. She supports me, but she doesn't attend my "pity parties." She is so good about reminding me to let go, probably because she's been there too.

*Listen to understand, not to respond.*

## Put the past behind you

My parents raised my brother and I with strict discipline and a lot of love. There were times I would declare my hatred for them in the moments of youth while my backside was still sore and the tears were still streaming. My mom was the worst because I was "daddy's little girl." When I was 12, my parents, led by my mother, became active in personal growth communities. I began to see fundamental changes in both of my parents as individuals and in my family as a whole.

When my mom and I *do* have an argument, we don't let it affect our future relationship. Having a constructive conversation and then putting it aside always proves to be more productive and rewarding then staying angry or hurt. I have also learned that out of breakdowns come breakthroughs. The process is challenging, but well worth it! Being able to move past and through our breakdowns is a strength we both take active roles in.

*Enjoy who she is now!*

## Enlightenment to who she really is

My mother has seen my development from the beginning. But she had a whole life before I came along. I don't know when I finally woke up to the fact that my mom was her own person, but it was a beautiful day. I remember visiting my grandparents as a teenager and discovering that my mom had saved several boxes of memorabilia from her younger years for her "someday daughter." My grandfather brought them out of the attic for me to look at. They were full of ticket stubs from plays she'd attended, matchbooks from restaurants she'd liked, programs and flyers from clubs she'd been involved with, anything French that she could get her hands on, and even some record albums.

In later years I began to ask her about her relationship with my dad and seek her dating advice. How have they made it over 30 years? She can't always completely relate to what I'm going through, but she listens and offers what advice she can. She is a role model for me and I value her life experiences.

*Know your mother for who she is, not just who you think she is. You can learn a lot, both about her and yourself.*

## Call them on their stuff

This is a very challenging role to take in someone's life. You need to know them very well and you need to have open communication. You must also be secure in your love for each other, so you can deal with the defenses they throw your way.

Too few people do this for me in my life. My mom is one of the few that can and does. She can call me on the games I play and the needless stress I put myself under. Over the years, I've learned to reciprocate the favor.

One of the situations that I've recently been able to help my mom through is my brother Dov's choice to live abroad. As a mother, she was having a hard time letting go. I got to listen to her and support her through this process. I also called her on her "stuff," each time she found a new "rationale" for why Dov should "come home." I helped her to see that it was her emotions, not her true beliefs, that were stopping her from embracing Dov's decision. I also reminded her that Dov was doing the same thing she had done when she chose to leave England and move to the United States.

Life is a challenging journey for all of us. Having someone who is willing and able to call you on your "stuff," and help you see a more balanced perspective is such a gift.

*Before change can happen, we must first be aware of a problem.*

# Touch each other often

Touch is good for your health, your heart, and your relationship. Touch is free, and readily available.

As a tactile individual and a massage therapist, I have embraced touch my entire life. When I'm separated from my family, I undergo bouts of touch deprivation and a part of me feels dead. Whenever I see my mom I make sure to get in some good snuggling time. I can't get enough of the head stroking, back rubs, and cuddling. I love it when we curl up in bed late at night for a movie or early in the morning after my dad's left for work. Touch is one of the most calming, reassuring, and relaxing gifts that we can give to one another.

Touch is also the first sense to function fully, and it plays a key role in the growth of our other senses. Touch produces a hormone called Oxytocin, which promotes bonding between parents and children and between mates. It rises in response to touch and in return promotes touching.

> *"Touch is your most precious and powerful resource.*
> *Don't underestimate it, and make sure to use it*
> *to your full advantage."*
>
> – Theresa L. Crenshaw, M.D.
> *The Alchemy of Love and Lust.*

When I sit back and look at what my mother and I have shared, and how much more is possible, I count my blessings. Honesty and respect can go a long way. Keep the channels of communication open and enjoy each other as you are!

\* \* \* \* \* \*

In Chapter Seven, you will learn the secrets of using crisis as a means for fulfilling your dreams.

# About Susan Friedmann, CSP

S usan works with organizations and individuals who want to fulfill their dreams and become masters of their destiny.

She works one-on-one and with teams to help boost results. She also conducts presentations and workshops nationally and internationally. She provides her clients with what they need to know to work together more effectively. She identifies and helps people develop the skills that are critical to their success now and in the future. She shows people how to build better relationships with customers, prospects, and advocates in the marketplace to retain and grow their business.

Originally from London, England, Susan has been a consultant, speaker, and author for over 15 years. Her extensive experience in business, particularly sales, marketing, and public relations, has allowed her to work with several hundred companies representing more than 30 different industries in the U.S. and in Europe.

As an innovative and insightful speaker, Susan has been featured at many major conventions and in the media. She is the author of 11 business books, including *Business Event Planning for Dummies*. She is also a regular contributing editor to numerous professional and trade publications.

Susan is an active member of the National Speakers Association, Certified Speaking Professional, former adjunct faculty member, San Francisco State University, former contract speaker for Fred Pryor Seminars, and a past president of the American Marketing Association — Cincinnati Chapter.

# Be the Master of Your Destiny!

Don't settle for anything less than all the fame and celebrity you want, all the income and wealth you want, all the success you want...

Being the master of your destiny means discovering your own ability to realize your noblest visions, values, and ideas. It is the possibility to transform yourself to achieve desired results by bringing about profound changes in thinking and behavior. In other words, getting what you want out of your life.

Being the master of your destiny allows you to unearth what you passionately care about, reach breakthrough goals, and implement transformational change. It provides you with the ideas, methods, and tools that enable you to make the difference you have always wanted to make.

*Sow an act, and you reap a habit.*
*Sow a habit, and you reap a character.*
*Sow a character, and you reap a destiny.*

– Charles Reade 1814-1884

# About Yael Friedmann, LMT

**Y**ael Friedmann is an educator, an artist, and a nationally certified massage therapist. As an innovative and creative thinker who loves to look at life from different perspectives, Yael is inspired about integrating the arts into education. She is pursuing her masters in art education at the Art Institute of Chicago.

A 1999 graduate of Hampshire College, Amherst, MA., Yael's studies focused on interdisciplinary education through the arts in middle schools. She was also a participant in Project Zero, a professional development workshop at Harvard Graduate School of Education. She has served as a museum educator at the Drawing Center, New York, N.Y., and the Museum Coordinator at Hebrew Union College, New York, N.Y. Currently, Yael is working with the Chicago Teacher's Center as a visiting artist helping teachers in the public schools with arts integration.

In addition to pursuing her inspired purpose, Yael delights in helping people to integrate their mind, body, and spirit through the art of massage therapy. She graduated from the Scherer Institute of Natural Healing in the autumn of 2000, after completing 760 hours of massage therapy education and training. She continued her studies with Oncology training and volunteer work at the New Mexico Oncology Clinic and earned her Level One certification in Reiki.

Yael has worked as a skilled medical massage therapist at Universal Health Institute, a holistic chiropractic care center in Chicago, IL. Currently, she maintains a private massage practice in which she incorporates a variety of massage modalities. Her clients credit her with being able to bring perspective and awareness to their body, mind, and spirit through her purposeful and healing touch.

# Yael Friedmann, LMT

## Nationally Certified Massage Therapist

Through her private practice, Yael offers a wide variety of massage modalities, including relaxation and stress release, sports massage, and therapeutic massage. She is also skilled in the use of massage techniques that incorporate hot rocks and energy work.

## Seminars Include:

### FIGURative Expression

This one-day workshop offers an interdisciplinary approach to the body, through the arts.

### Healing Hands

During this half-day workshop, participants learn basic massage techniques that they can put to personal use. They also learn how to integrate the body, mind, and spirit, while performing a self-massage, or massaging a friend or family member.

For more information or to make an appointment
for a private massage, contact Yael at
773-354-3116
yada123@yahoo.com

# CHAPTER SEVEN

# Crisis as a Means for Fulfilling Your Dreams

*by*
*Dr. Esther Konigsberg*

# Crisis as a Means for Fulfilling Your Dreams

Dr. Esther Konigsberg

---

*"Your joy is your sorrow unmasked."*

– Kahlil Gibran

---

Have you ever asked, "Why did this have to happen to me?" Perhaps your relationship ended, you lost your job, faced a chronic or life-threatening illness, or experienced the loss of a loved one. At that time the world might have seemed like a very unfair place.

At some point, everyone faces crises such as these. We often carry the wounds from these life-altering events for months, years, or perhaps the rest of our life. We feel scarred and find it difficult to engage in life: trust new relationships, feel safe in our new jobs, believe in our bodies' healing capacity, and open our hearts to love.

Wouldn't it be amazing to find a way to make sense of it all? To find the blessing in the crisis? Many of us have met or heard about people who have faced monumental crises and have become thankful for the experience. I have been fortunate to know many such individuals.

One of my patients, Kimberly, a 28-year-old teacher, suddenly became a widow when she lost her husband in a hiking accident. Over the next 16 months, she lost both her parents to cancer. As a result of her losses, she decided to take a sabbatical from teaching and re-entered University in a masters program for religion and theology. Kimberly tells me that her life has become much more meaningful as she shares her knowledge, faith, and experiences with her students and her fiancé. Kimberly has found her life's purpose.

So how can we be like Kimberly? How can we find the meaning in a life crisis? Is it even possible to find our life's purpose as a consequence of our experience? The answer is yes! The following insights and tools will assist you to find meaning in crisis, enable you to transform crisis into blessing, and help you become aware of your life purpose.

## Remaining Present in Crisis

A crisis is a turning point or decisive moment, a time of acute danger or suspense. It stands to reason that many of us find crisis stressful. Our minds and bodies react to stress through the fight or flight response, also called the stress response.

The fight or flight response has been hard-wired in our bodies since ancient times and is particularly useful during life-threatening emergencies. When our ancestors faced a saber-toothed tiger, their bodies became flooded with stress hormones, adrenaline, and cortisol, which in turn increased their blood pressure, heart rate, and breathing rate so that blood and energy flowed into their brains and muscles, making them hyper-alert and capable of either fighting the tiger or fleeing for their lives.

During a life crisis we often feel as if we're in "acute danger or suspense" for considerable lengths of time. During this time the stress response is repeatedly triggered. Continued release of the stress hormones leads to anxiety, feelings of overwhelm, depression, high blood pressure, heart disease, irritable bowel syndrome, poor immunity (infections, cancer), headaches, and insomnia, to name a few.

Mary, a 55-year old patient of mine felt trapped in her job as a personal banker. Over the years her company had increased its demands and she was now expected to handle almost twice her initial workload. She came in to see me complaining of headaches, indigestion, and insomnia. She found it hard to concentrate as her mind was always racing. Mary depended on her income and didn't see any alternatives, "because I'm too old and no one else will hire me."

Mary's stress response was so heightened that it immobilized her from coming up with creative responses to her situation. She needed some tools to counteract the stress response. I taught her two powerful techniques for reversing the stress response: The Calming Breath and Mindfulness Meditation.

## The Calming Breath

Conscious breathing has a calming influence on the mind and body. Changing the rate and depth of breathing releases endorphins, the body's natural opiates, which counteract adrenaline and cortisol, the stress hormones.

Find a quiet, private place to perform this breathing exercise. A comfortable chair allows you to sit upright with your back straight and both feet on the floor. If you don't have a private place available, a bathroom will do. Keep your eyes closed while performing this technique.

1. Using your right hand, position your thumb beside your right nostril and your middle two fingers beside your left nostril.

2. Gently close the right nostril with your thumb and slowly exhale through your left nostril. Inhale easily through your left nostril.

3. Release your thumb from the right nostril and gently close the left nostril with your fingers. Exhale and inhale easily through your right nostril.

4. Alternate nostrils for five minutes allowing your breath to come naturally but a little slower and deeper than usual.

5. When finished, keep your eyes closed and concentrate on the sensations in your body for one to two minutes. You may notice a pleasant lightness in the head or a warm vibrating energy within.

Never strain during this exercise. If you feel uncomfortable, stop and breathe normally until the sensation passes and try the exercise again. Try this technique the next time you feel "stressed out." You may notice a calming effect after only a few minutes.

### *Mindfulness Meditation*

Meditation reverses and helps to prevent the stress response. Scientific studies have demonstrated that regular meditators have decreased levels of circulating stress hormones and increased levels of antidepressant hormones such as serotonin and dopamine in their bloodstreams. The stress-related illnesses I mentioned are improved by regular meditation. The immune system becomes enhanced which means fewer colds and infections.

Meditation reverses biological age markers, which means it helps to slow the aging process. Meditation improves your energy level, mental alertness, concentration, and learning ability. Meditation is like taking Prozac without popping a pill. As a result, things that previously caused stress just don't anymore. You will find yourself living in the moment and appreciating it.

Practice Mindfulness Meditation while sitting comfortably in a quiet room with your eyes closed. Simply allow your awareness to be on your breath without trying to alter the breath in any way. As thoughts or bodily sensations come and go, just keep bringing your awareness back to your breathing. Gradually, the flow of thoughts becomes interrupted and your mind becomes silent. For the best results, practice this meditation technique for 20-30 minutes twice daily.

The Calming Breath and Mindfulness Meditation are two very effective tools to use during stressful times. They will help bring a sense of calm and present moment awareness. As a result, you will be better equipped to look for the hidden blessings in each and every situation.

Mary was able to incorporate these wonderful tools into her life, which enabled her to relax and calm her mind and increased her ability to focus in the present. Her physical symptoms improved and she became much more productive in her job. With her mind focused in the present, Mary was able to find opportunities to creatively solve her situation. She consciously decided to make a change and eventually found an interesting job within the bank at a smaller branch with fewer demands. Mary feels that her experience has benefited her greatly. She had to take stock of her life and decide on her priorities. Although she has a slightly smaller paycheck, she said, "I'm better able to appreciate my life in each and every moment. A feeling that's priceless to me!"

# Transforming Crisis into Blessing

Now that you have tools for reversing stress and becoming present during times of crisis, you can begin to find the benefits and opportunities in even the most difficult situations. There is a technique for transforming crisis into blessing and all you need is a pen and paper.

Sit in a quiet room where you won't have any distractions. Perform the Calming Breath for two to five minutes. Now draw a line down the middle of the page. On the right side of the page, at the top, write: "If my life and circumstances had stayed the same as they were before this crisis, (divorce, job change, etc.) what would the drawbacks be to me?" On the left side of the page write, "What benefits and opportunities have happened and do I foresee happening as a result of this crisis?"

List at least 10 answers for each question. The answers may not seem obvious and forthcoming at first, but with some deep thought and perseverance I guarantee they will begin to flow.

Let me provide an example that may help you in this process. Stacy had been married one year when her husband Brian was diagnosed with a brain tumor. Devastated by the news, their relationship became even closer. Brian underwent aggressive medical therapy, which eventually drove the disease into remission. They both decided to "get on with their lives," and Stacy became pregnant. A few months before the baby was due, Brian had a recurrence and received more therapy but was left with a mild leg paralysis.

The baby was born three weeks early with Brian in joyful attendance at the delivery. Unfortunately Brian suffered a massive blood clot to his lungs three weeks later on the baby's actual due date and died instantly. A new mother and widow almost simultaneously, Stacey "fell apart." She moved back in with her parents for almost a year. Eventually, she went back to work, got involved in team sports, and began dating.

Stacy still felt a deep anger about losing Brian and was sometimes very depressed about her life being "much harder" as a result of this loss. She used the Transformation Technique to further her healing.

This is how Stacy's process went:

"If my life and circumstances had stayed the same as they were before Brian's illness and death, what would the drawbacks be to me?"

1. I was dependent on Brian and my family.

2. I had low self-esteem.

3. I was a worrywart.

4. I worried about what people thought about me.

5. I tried to please people even at the expense of myself.

6. My relationships were superficial.

7. Once we had a family, I would have stayed home while Brian worked long hours.

8. Things were easy. I wasn't challenged and therefore I wasn't growing.

9. I worked hard for the future and didn't pay enough attention to living in the present.

10. I was easily affected by the little things and didn't appreciate my life as much as I should have.

"What benefits and opportunities have happened and do I foresee happening as a result of this crisis?"

1. I have become more compassionate.

2. I feel much stronger and have become a capable problem solver.

3. I have become a good listener and have deeper relationships with my friends, family, and clients.

4.  I have a strong sense of myself and have become capable of expressing my values and staying true to them.

5.  I am much more passionate about my work as a travel agent. I know that when I sell vacations, I help create meaningful life experiences for my clients.

6.  As a single mother I have created a very strong and nurturing relationship with my son.

7.  I love reading and learning about the challenges and mysteries of life and about the human spirit.

8.  I get tremendous feedback and support from all sorts of people in my life who say they respect me for how I have handled my life's challenges.

9.  I cherish and appreciate my relationships much more than ever before.

10. I understand that every moment is precious and the little things seldom bother me.

After Stacy completed this Transformation Technique, she felt a shift in how she viewed the past few years and her present life circumstances. She realized that through Brian's illness and death, she had experienced a profound personal growth and evolution and had found much more meaning in her life.

Stacy was able to see the many blessings from her crisis and transform the anger and depression into love and gratitude for her life as it is. Now, she is enjoying mothering her son, excelling in her career, and is in a serious relationship with a "beautiful man."

# Discovering Life Purpose Through Crisis

Crisis can inspire us to find a deeper meaning in our lives, to find our life's purpose. We are pursuing our life's purpose when we passionately do what we love to do with present moment awareness. When we follow our purpose, we grow and evolve and help others to do the same. Our life's purpose is much more than a job. It's an inspired inner knowing of what we feel called to do in this lifetime.

There are numerous examples of people finding their life's purpose through crisis. There are many individuals whose lives have been touched by AIDS, drunk drivers, drugs, incest, etc. who speak to the public to raise awareness and prevent the repetition of similar crises in the lives of others:

➤ Priscilla de Villiers, mother of Nina de Villiers, who was shot and killed by a man on parole several years ago, became instrumental in changing Canadian law to better protect its citizens.

➤ Dr.Rachel Naomi Remen, best selling author of *Kitchen Table Wisdom* and *My Grandfather's Blessings*, who has Crohn's disease, inspires her patients and the public to find the blessings in their physical challenges.

➤ Dr. Deepak Chopra, who has been called the poet/prophet of alternative medicine, started his spiritual journey when he began meditating to help him quit smoking.

➤ The list is endless...

Here are two techniques to help you accelerate the process of discovering your life's purpose through crisis:

1. Sit in a comfortable position and close your eyes. Practice the Calming Breath for two minutes, then silently ask yourself, "What is my life's purpose?" If an answer pops up immediately, make a mental note of it and let it go.

   Begin your Mindfulness Meditation and let go of the question. Often, the answer bubbles up during meditation or later when you're in the midst of activity. You will know in your heart if you have become aware of your life purpose, as you will be filled with inspiration.

2.  Sit in a quiet room with a pen and paper. Practice the Calming Breath for two to five minutes. Write at least three answers for each of the following questions:

> ➤ How has this crisis enriched my life and enhanced my personal growth?

> ➤ What unique talents have I gained as a result of this crisis?

> ➤ How can I passionately share my newly gained insights and talents with others so that I may assist in the evolution of our planet?

I would like to share my own story to help illustrate the power of this process. Approximately eight years ago, I was a family physician, wife, and mother of three young children, when my husband told me that he had been sexually involved with an employee in his medical office, who also happened to be his patient. Not only did I feel personally devastated, but I was also fearful of my husband losing his license to practice medicine and the publicity that might follow.

Within a week of this crisis, I heard an interview of Dr. Deepak Chopra and was immediately inspired. Over the next eight years, while dealing with my husband's depression, my marriage, a public hearing, and local newspaper publicity, I personally embarked on a mental, vocational, and spiritual journey. I read books, listened to tapes, attended courses and seminars, and became certified to teach meditation and mind/body health. I began speaking and teaching widely about health and spirituality as well as being featured extensively in the media.

Here is how using the process for finding life's purpose worked for me:

1. I asked myself before meditation, "What is my life's purpose?" The answer which repeatedly came to me was "to help create a new form of health care which honors the mind, body, and spirit."

2. With pen and paper, I answered the following three questions as follows:

    i) *How has this crisis enriched my life and enhanced my personal growth?*

    ➤ I entered into therapy with my husband, which has not only helped our relationship, but has also allowed me to become increasingly conscious of my own behaviors and transform them.

    ➤ I have become a passionate student of life.

    ➤ I feel more deeply connected to the universal web of life.

    ii) *What unique talents have I gained as a result of this crisis?*

    ➤ I have become a skilled instructor in meditation and mind/body medicine.

    ➤ I have become aware of the blessings in challenging situations and maintain a balanced and broader perspective.

    ➤ I have become a more knowledgeable and skilful communicator, speaker, and writer.

iii) *How can I passionately share my newly gained insights and talents with others, so that I may assist in the evolution of our planet?*

➤ Through interactions with my family, friends, and patients.

➤ Through teaching courses, speaking, and writing.

➤ Through helping to establish a Centre in Integrated Medicine incorporating different healing arts and sciences to honor, support, and heal our patients/clients, minds, bodies, and spirits. (This is a long-term goal.)

The past 8 years have brought so much depth and meaning to my life. My greatest sorrow has been the source of my greatest joy. Beyond sorrow, beyond joy, I experience unbelievable fulfillment as my life's purpose continues to unfold. I feel deep love and gratitude for my journey and my life as it is.

I am certain that when you use these extraordinary techniques, you will transform crisis into an opportunity for growth, evolution, and the fulfillment of your unique life's purpose. You will be filled with love and gratitude for your life as it was, as it is, and as it continues to be.

\* \* \* \* \* \*

In Chapter Eight, explore the powerful connections between musical vibrations and your spirit.

# About Dr. Esther Konigsberg

D r. Esther Konigsberg is a dedicated Family Physician, mind/body wellness educator, meditation instructor, seminar leader, speaker, and writer. She has studied extensively with world leaders in health, healing, spirituality, and human potential including Dr. Deepak Chopra, Dr. David Simon, Dr. John F. Demartini, and Dr. Andrew Weil.

Dr. Konigsberg began to pursue her life-long interest in Mind/Body medicine at McGill University where she obtained her Bachelor of Science in Physiological Psychology in 1980 and a Medical Degree at McMaster University in 1983. As well as being a member of the Canadian College of Family Physicians, she is currently enrolled in the Associate Fellowship Program in Integrative Medicine at the University of Arizona.

Dr. Konigsberg has been leading transformational seminars and lecturing widely to both the public and corporate world since 1996. She has written numerous magazine and newspaper articles on mind, body, and spirit health and healing. She has been interviewed and featured on television and radio talk shows as well as newspapers and magazines including "Chatelaine" and "Newsweek."

Dr. Konigsberg is actively practicing Family Medicine in Burlington, Ontario, where she lives with her husband and three children.

# Infinite Health

**Dr. Esther Konigsberg**
3067 Balmoral Avenue
Burlington, Ontario Canada
L7N 1E5
905-632-2220
infin8health@hotmail.com

## Services:

➤ Personal Consultations

➤ Speaking Engagements

➤ Customized workshops and seminars for groups, businesses, and organizations

## Seminars Include:

### Creating Health

A five-lesson program for physical, mental, and spiritual well-being. Developed by Drs. Deepak Chopra and David Simon, this course provides the tools to enhance your physical and emotional vitality. These tools include; mindfulness meditation, nourishment for body, mind, and soul, eliminating toxins, healing through the senses, and emotional cleansing.

### Primordial Sound Meditation

A weekend or three-session course designed to introduce or deepen the meditation experience. Primordial sounds are nature's sounds incorporated into a personalized mantra (a silently repeated sound) based on the participant's place, date, and time of birth. Designed by Dr. Deepak Chopra, this course will help you discover the silence which creates inner peace and renews energy for the challenges of daily living.

## Mind, Body and Spirit in the Workplace: An Investment in Employee Transformation

This three-hour, on-site program, introduces employees to the basic mind/ body/spirit concepts in a group work setting. These fundamental techniques, meditation, breathing exercises, and emotional clearing, will reduce stress and enhance relationships. You can augment this introduction with other modules at a later date.

## Crisis: Finding Meaning and Growth Through Life-Altering Events

This three-hour course provides practical techniques for finding personal growth and transformation through crisis. This course teaches participants how to remain present in the midst of a crisis, to transform crisis into blessing, and to discover their life purpose through crisis.

To learn more about seminars and services,
or for speaking engagements, contact
Dr. Esther Konigsberg at Infinite Health.

# CHAPTER EIGHT

# From Quanta to Cosmos, Vibrations of Music and Our Spirit

*by*
*Robert Mari*

# From Quanta to Cosmos, Vibrations of Music and Our Spirit

Robert Mari

---

*"The rotation of the universe and the motion of the planets could neither begin nor continue without music...for everything is ordered by God according to the laws of harmony."*

– Plutarch

## Prelude

What do the Milky Way Galaxy, our solar system, the moon, the earth's rotation, our human hearts, and each quanta that makes up the atoms in every molecule in our bodies all have in common?

Cycles. They flow and vibrate in a periodic manner, each with its own frequency.

Have you ever thought about all the cycles that surround us? Let's start with our heart that is beating a constant rhythm in conjunction with our lungs breathing in and out throughout the cycle of our life. The sun rises and sets each day within the moon month and the seasons of each year. We are part of this harmony of the universe, vibrating with it. Music, too, is filled with layers of cycles and can help us align with our spirit and open our hearts to the genius within. By learning to understand and "map" these cycles in music, your music selections can create a "vibrational" bridge from where you are — to where you'd love to be. If we appreciate and learn which pieces of music touch our hearts and consciousness, we can break through to a more fulfilling life.

# We are Naturally Harmonious

*"There is geometry in the humming of the strings.*
*There is music in the spacing of the spheres."*

– Pythagoras

Harmony in music is simply shifting patterns of different tones through simultaneous or implied juxtaposition. In other words, musical harmony is created from layers of notes (vibrations or cycles).

There are many layers of cycles in our life. Starting at the minutest level and the quickest frequency of vibration, some quantum physicists believe the source of all energy and matter in the universe is one-dimensional vibration. At a slower vibration, yet still very fast, are the cycles of molecules humming in our bodies and the crystals in our watches. Then there are the cycles of our bodies: heart beating, walking, breathing, regeneration of our cells, and our life.

Next, let's look to the sky for the cycles of our solar system. There is the earth day and lunar month and the year it takes us to circle the sun. Then there are huge cycles at the galactic level, such as the solar system going around the center of the Milky Way galaxy and the galaxy itself rotating around in the local cluster of galaxies!

All these cycles vibrate together in the beautiful harmony of a grand choir, like ripples on ocean waves clapping the beach while dancing within the tides.

# Talking Waves!

*"After silence, that which comes nearest to expressing the inexpressible, is music."*

– Aldous Huxley

Music has many layers of vibrations and cycles, but before exploring those layers, I'd like to explain how information is communicated through vibrations. There is a phenomenon called sympathetic reverberation. This is what happens when a singer breaks a glass by singing the correct note. If you sing into a guitar, you'll notice that the strings of the guitar vibrate. What's happening is that the vibrations of your voice are transmitted to the strings, thereby affecting and energizing them. Why is this important? If this happens to something as simple as a guitar string, what about all the vibrations that we come into contact with every day of our life? The seasons, as well as the time of day affect us. We also respond to music.

Information can be stored and communicated on top of waves. A clear example is radio waves. Let's suppose that you are in your car and radio station KRVM is broadcasting your favorite piece of music. You tune the radio to the particular frequency KRVM is broadcasting. The car radio is receiving information stored on radio waves (lower frequency electromagnetic light/ waves) and decoding that information to its speakers. The air then carries the vibrations from the speakers and transmits it to your ears, which sympathetically vibrate like the guitar strings. Your ears decode those vibrations into bio-chemical reactions transmitting the information along nerves to your brain creating the thought "ah, my favorite song!"

Each radio wave has a single frequency, such as 102.5 kHz. Yet, infused on each wave is the information that gets decoded into the sounds we hear. On the wave itself are layers of information. Cycles on top of cycles: Harmony.

# Harmonic Layers

*"Do you know that our soul is composed of harmony?"*

– Leonardo da Vinci

Let's explore the many layers of music and then I'll relate them to the sympathetic vibrations within us that get activated by being exposed to music.

A note of music has a frequency ranging from 20 cycles per second (cps) to 25,000 cps. They are all fast enough that we experience them as tones. These tones vibrate at frequencies that resonate with the cells in our bodies. Our eardrums also vibrate sympathetically to these tones and transmit the information to our brains.

Another layer of music is the rhythm. This is the dance layer: you know, one-two-three-four, left-right-left-right. Rhythm in music vibrates at cycles or beats per minute and resonates with our heart and the pace of our walking. Not only does the rhythm of this layer communicate to our feet and legs, but our hearts will try to synchronize sympathetically to the beat of the music.

Another longer rhythm of the music is the harmony, and it usually changes every 2 to 8 beats. These structures change in familiar patterns and can be likened to the words in sentences.

The next slower and longer cycle of music is the phrase. This is typically between 8 and 32 beats of music and it corresponds with our breath. This is in part due to making the music natural to sing (it takes about one breath to sing a phrase of music.) This cycle is similar in length to a sentence that corresponds to a thought. Therefore each phrase of music typically communicates a single thought.

The last cycle of music is the piece itself. It has its own unique life cycle of being born into the air, breathing and dancing and uniting with us until all that remains is its essence buried in the memory of our soul.

In summary, music is communicating to us at high vibrations at the electro-chemical level, slower vibrations at the physical, and still slower vibrations at the thought and memory layer. Like a radio station sending its signals into the ether, the musician transmits and encodes all the layers of music to each of us. We then become the radios that decode the message into emotions and thoughts in sympathetic response.

# Riding the Waves

*"That which cannot be expressed otherwise*
*can only be told through music.*
*A thought, which seems commonplace in*
*its analysis, acquires a deeper sense in music."*

– Tagore

Let's experience the communication process. Read the following poem and notice the 5 different inflections of *warm*.

### Warmth
### by Robert Mari

returning from a barren sleep, greeted by spring's warmth
still yearning for your presence and warm touch
children at play, laughing eyes, warm rosy cheeks
returning to bed, cuddled with down's protective warmth

in gratitude, grace, my soul speaks the sun's warmth

Although the word *warm* is repeated five times, the surrounding images of each line release fresh nuances of meaning in the word. When I play the piano I only have 88 keys! Not only that, but there are really only 12 notes repeated at different octaves. Think about the fact that for centuries of music we continue to have unique and fresh combinations of those 12 notes.

Let's look at a musical example that takes a few notes through many transformations. A piece of mine called *Arrival* (to listen to this piece, refer to the end of this chapter) has three notes repeated twice over five different harmonic structures — just like *warm* in the poem. In fact, I wrote the poem modeling it on the opening tune of *Arrival*. So even if you don't listen to the music, the following will apply to both (poem references are in parenthesis, just like this). This means that you hear the same three notes played 30 times — 3x2 by 5.

Each of the five harmonic structures (lines of the poem) gives these same notes (the word *warmth*) a fresh emotional response. The first is bright and cheery. The second turns to longing. Next it brightens with joyful playfulness before it prepares to settle down (fourth). And finally, fifth, we arrive in harmony with the universe. All these swings happen in the short 42-second opening of the piece.

What is it that makes it possible for all this imagery and emotion to be conveyed so efficiently? First and foremost it is memory. We have heard patterns of words and music millions of times. These patterns, through repetition, build meanings from associations. In other words, each pattern is like a single wave of a radio with information encoded into it. The word *warmth* in the poem has the encoded data stimulated and released by the surrounding words. The three-note melody also has its impressions released, based on its placement in the familiar harmony of the structure surrounding it. This is possible only if the listener has stored some kind of memory that has associations that can be stimulated.

Another reason that the music communicates to us is the tension and relaxation of the vibrations of the notes in relationship to the surrounding harmony. This provides various levels of concord/discord. Finally, when the performer combines the change in dynamics, sensitivity, and placement of the rhythm, the final expression (information) has been added to the resonance (vibration) of the music.

# Mapping

*"Within music lies all the wonders and keys
to the miracles of life — natural and spiritual.
Music can facilitate the process of change and growth."*
– Ted Andrews

Before we proceed, list five special pieces of music. Select pieces that you particularly like and that have moved you to a deep and special experience.

1. _____

2. _____

3. _____

4. _____

5. _____

No two people experience a piece of music the same way. Nor do we experience the same piece the same way every time.

The sympathetic vibrations that we experience depend on our own personal vibrations at that moment. We can, however, generalize and map what a piece of music tends to elicit. The following map allows us to describe the areas and direction that a piece of music explores as it unfolds.

# Robert's Map of Music Territory

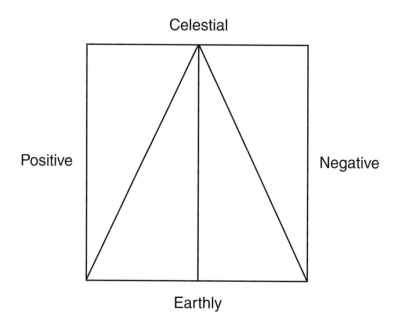

Celestial

Positive

Negative

Earthly

Toward the left side of the map (west) are the emotions you experience to the music when it is positive, happy, and pleasant. Toward the right (east) are negative, sad, and painful emotions. The top/bottom axis (north/south) is not about emotions. Instead this axis represents our interpretation of the substance of the music. Is it earthly, physical, or heavy, down south, or is it ethereal, spiritual, or transcendent toward the north?

Some pieces of music stay in one area of the map for the duration. For instance, I find Motets (choral pieces) by the 16th Century composer Giovanni Pierluigi da Palestrina to be at the top center of the map: celestial with a perfect, beautiful balance of harmony from beginning to end. While rap music, with its intricate strong, repeated rhythm and ultra-simple harmony stays earthy and physical for the duration. I experience my piece *Arrival* as staying fairly close to the center of the map until about two-thirds of the way through when it climaxes to a soulful peak before settling down again.

Other music can traverse great and varied landscapes of the map. Beethoven's 6th, 7th or 9th Symphonies are good examples of pieces that take us on a journey from earthly pain or fear, to pleasant meadows, to celestial tranquility or triumph. My own variations on the children's tune *Twinkle Twinkle* starts in the center left of the map works its way to the bottom left, then winds over to the middle right before emerging to the top center. (See end of chapter for methods of hearing this piece.)

For me to experience personal growth from music, a variety of music that guides me to the center top of the map is most effective. There have also been occasions when fantastic Cuban rhythms (bottom left) or the intense emotional love of Wagner's *Tristan und Isolde* (mid-center) have prepared me for deeply inspirational ideas.

# Time to Map

*"Music is a higher revelation than
all wisdom or philosophy."*

– Beethoven

Learning to map music is one of the secrets to tuning into your emotions, instincts, and inspirations. By mapping and noting the response that you have to various pieces of music, you can choose the music that will carry you to the place on the map where you wish to go.

Take some time to listen to the pieces you listed above and map them on paper. When the piece begins, place your pen on the map. I find that a soft medium point felt pen works best. It allows me to express intensity by pressing harder, thus increasing the thickness of the line and adding a third dimension to the map. As the music progresses, see if you find your response to the music changing. Move the pen to the location on the map as you notice it change. If you have difficulty placing the pen, not knowing where to start, just pick a place that seems close.

Reflect on the following questions:

➤ Does your pen move from one place to another on the map even though the music has not changed? (You are synchronizing to the music.)

➤ Are you staying in the same place even though the music is going through changes? (Perhaps the music doesn't seem to resonate with you or your attention is elsewhere.)

➤ Are you being pulled and guided to different areas? (The music is taking you on a journey.)

➤ After mapping all your pieces, is there something that you can learn from reviewing the maps?

➤ Do your maps tell you something about the music that you find fulfilling?

# Tuning into a Higher Channel

*"The art of music is endowed with a supernatural origin and a divine purpose, more so than any other art."*

– Leibniz

Notice the diagonal lines that form a triangle on the map. I place these lines as guides for music that takes us on a journey away from our physical reality to that of the spirit. By ascending to the top of the pyramid we vibrate in a state that opens us up to communicate more clearly with our true self.

The following exercise can help you to find answers to questions and to receive inspirational messages that will help you to break through to a more fulfilling life.

First, find music that takes you on the journey to the top center of the map. Some musical pieces that I find particularly centering are: Choral Motets by Palestrina; Indian sitar music by Ravi Shankar; Mozart's *Requiem*; and Samuel Barbers *Adagio for Strings*. Many people have commented that my CD *Arrival* takes them to that special place.

➤ Before listening to the music, sit in a comfortable chair that is placed an equal distance from each of the speakers. If possible, you should be at the tip of an equal sided triangle with the speakers at the other corners.

➤ Sit quietly for a few minutes and clear your mind of any disturbing thoughts. Center your mind on inner peace. As you do this, start breathing through your nostrils in a regular rhythm.

➤ When you feel centered, start the music. As it plays, keep breathing through your nose and breathe in and out in tempo with the music. Allow yourself to become centered with the sounds.

➤ When the music is over, sit in silence and open your mind to receive the answers to your questions or the inspirational thoughts that await your consciousness. Write down everything that comes to you and thank your higher self for your blessings.

# Finale

*"Real music is not for wealth, not for honors
or even the joys of the mind … but is a path
for realization and salvation."*

– Ali Akbar Khan

Beethoven said, "Music is the soil in that the spirit lives, thinks, and invents." I believe that music is the vibration of everything in the universe. I sincerely hope that you will take advantage of its power and let it vibrate in you, so you can break through, open your heart, and release the greatness that lies within. May your light shine. May your heart sing.

## Music Samples

To listen to *Arrival* and *Twinkle Twinkle,* go to http://www.syntonicarts.com. If you do not have Internet access, you can request a CD or Tape of these music samples by sending a letter to: Syntonic Arts, PO Box 5655, Station B, Victoria, B.C. Canada, V8S 6S4.

\* \* \* \* \* \*

In Chapter Nine, discover the hero that lies within.

# About Robert Mari

Robert began studying music at age three. At thirteen, he began learning Universal Principles by studying science, religions, and psychology. By sixteen, he had become Musical Director, Arranger, and Conductor for two Russian Folk Orchestras. He studied music formally and holds Bachelor and Master of Music degrees. While studying for a Doctorate of Musical Arts at the Peabody Institute of The Johns Hopkins University, he became proficient with computers. He later drew on that proficiency in establishing his international consulting business.

Robert's ten-year exploration of electronic music and subsequent return to acoustic instruments gave him his first taste of the mystical states accessible through direct, in-the-moment immersion in live music. Today he opens hearts and inspires people to greater consciousness through his expression on piano, orchestral conducting, composition, sculpture, and art. He also loves being on the edge of the moment through improvised stream-of-consciousness performance. As a multi-disciplinary artist, he aspires to communicate the song of unconditional love in his heart to a worldwide audience.

Robert founded Syntonic Arts to enable the creation of works of art that synthesize sound (music), light (art, sculpture, visual lights) and movement (dance, robotics, mobiles) into single works (opus), installation pieces, movie soundtracks, or performances, to open people's hearts to the genius within.

**SyntonicArts**

Syntonic Arts enables the creation of artistic works that synthesize sound, light, and movement to open people's hearts to the genius within. *Syntonic* means in harmony with the environment and Syntonic's offerings include stirring performances, installation pieces, sculptures, original recordings, and personal counseling — all to help people find greater harmony in their lives.

Syntonic's artists include Robert Mari and various ensembles that Robert forms with people of exceptional creative talent. Syntonic's product offerings include Robert's moving debut commercial solo recording, *Arrival*, Robert and Jaime Taylor's timeless *A Note for Christmas*, and more. For an up-to-date list, music samples, artist news, and performance dates, visit www.syntonicarts.com Personal counseling by Robert Mari includes The Quantum Collapse Process™, transformations, and lectures.

Syntonic Arts is a division of Syntonic Ventures Ltd.

**Syntonic Arts**
Box 5655, Station B
Victoria, BC, V8R 6S4
www.syntonicarts.com

e-mail info@syntonic.com
(250)592-9893 or toll-free (866)592-9893

# CHAPTER NINE

# A Walk in the Park: The Importance of Heroes

*by*
*Dr. Amelia Case*

# A Walk in the Park: The Importance of Heroes

Dr. Amelia Case

---

*"And you'll finally see the truth,
that a hero lies in you."*

– "Hero" by Walter Afanasieff and Mariah Carey

---

I was walking in a beautiful Pennsylvania park with some of my best friends. I had flown in to visit because I was stressed. I was down. I was out. I needed help. A quiet weekend in this small town was the ticket.

We sat on a hill overlooking a long row of weeping willows. Off to our left several children were casting their fishing lines into the grass for practice. A younger boy was urging an older boy to let him take the rod, but the older boy wouldn't give it up. I looked at them, then looked away, half listening to the two boys argue. I sat, breathing the fresh country air with nothing on my mind. I was aware of the children, but not bothered by their disagreement. On the contrary, their exchange seemed part of the scene of a neighborhood park; it felt comfortable too.

I looked back at the small group of fishermen just in time to see the younger boy marching away from the rest of them. He picked his feet up faster, began to run, and then, as if in slow motion, he ran into the road — and under a moving truck. The driver screeched to a halt. Unfortunately, he stopped the truck right on top of the boy. People were shouting and screaming. Neighbors and other children ran in circles; some didn't move at all, paralyzed by panic. And there the truck sat, parked on top of the child. A neighbor was standing stiff on the side of the street crying out, "Oh, My God."

I ran as fast as I could, first to the truck-driver, commanding him to back up. It seemed like forever before the truck finally backed off of the boy, leaving the little guy lying there crying and moaning. I jumped over the top of him, told him my name, and said that I would help him. Then, for some odd reason, I questioned him.

"Do you remember Arnold Schwarzenegger, the Terminator? How he was messed-up? Do you remember?"

He looked me right in the eyes, stopped all motion, and said, calmly, "Yes."

"Well," I said, "You're messed-up. Just like Arnold, and you're gonna be okay, but you've gotta be fixed-up first. Are you with me?" He was. "Now, you have to help me fix you up."

Once his mind was focused on the Terminator, he was okay. Everything wasn't so scary. At the moment he identified with his hero, he was able to deal with the pain and chaos of what was happening. Actually, he seemed to be focused on the fact that he was messed-up. It interested him. When his parents arrived, *he* calmed his mother. He told her that he just had to get "fixed up."

As it turned out, he had suffered a fracture and dislocation of his pelvis and hip, and he has since recovered from his injuries very well. That little boy's name is Jared. He made my walk in the park the least relaxing but most rewarding walk I have ever taken.

What gives us courage on a day like that? For Jared, it was a composite of Arnold Schwarzenegger and the Terminator. All of the mental and emotional details of his hero congealed to form an image that either kept him company, kept him pre-occupied, or — based on what I observed — turned *him* into his hero. He had an example to follow. He was doing what Arnold would do. He transformed himself into the Terminator Boy and became calm, confident, and poised.

# A Hero Is a Powerful and Necessary Companion

Prior to my experience with Jared, I was flailing about like a victim on the pavement of life. I suffered one of those periods in life when every day hailed a new disaster. When I looked at myself in the mirror, I saw lifeless eyes looking back at me. I just wanted to go back to bed. After countless hours spent on advice, education, and therapy, I was still moving numbly through each day. Jared helped me realize that I was neglecting a missing ingredient: Knowing that I wasn't alone, and that I could get through it just like someone else did.

Knowing that someone else "went through it" helps us realize that we can persevere. Admiring someone for getting through a difficult time adds the special elements of interest and inspiration to go forward through a challenge. Jared is the little angel who showed me what I was missing — my hero. I could transform into my heroic self too.

We hold our heroes on a pedestal because they elevate us. They make our eyes fill with tears because they thrust us toward our best. Our heroes make us cry happy tears because we appreciate knowing that *we can do what they can do.* They help us to know our possibilities, see past our own assumed limitations, and give us hope that we can rise up. Our heroes inspire us. When we watch or listen to them, we feel our chests are filled with air. We breathe in, and find ourselves energized.

The kind of energy we get from our heroes is called inspiration. I love that word. I love the most simple meaning of it: the idea of standing up straight, tilting my head back, looking up to the sky and drawing in a great big breath. Feeling saturated with life's force...and animated. There is a strength and power to being inspired. That's when we light up with an idea, purpose, or plan. We feel alive. Inspiration exalts us and we crave it. Once touched by the most divine and supernatural experience, we are able to endure and accomplish all things.

## Heroes Guide Us to Our Inspiration

People are looking hard for inspiration in order to find meaning to who they are and what they do. The truth is that inspiration is never far away. I assure you that you can find inspiration anywhere, anytime, if you put your mind to noticing it. It's especially simple if you allow your hero to lead the way.

Bruce Jenner, the track and field decathlete and gold medal winner of the '76 Olympics in Montreal knew he could excel if he could see it. Photographs of his track and field heroes were posted on the walls around him, with one special change: a picture of his head was pasted on their bodies. He was inspired by his heroes and imagined himself as a famous decathlete. The photos reminded him that he could do what they did; he *would* do what they did. Bruce Jenner put his heroes to work for him. And when he stood on the podium to receive his gold medals, he was not alone. His heroes were with him.

# Inspiration Is the Secret to Motivation

We are meant to *do* something with our inspiration. We are designed to transform ourselves from one stage in life to another. We weren't born to just *be* inspired. The frontal lobes of our brains are meant for action. Our senses give us cause to express and act. The muscles in our arms and legs are meant to move. Inspiration is the secret to helping us become what we are meant to be. It's the secret key to motivate. Each one of us has been given a life's mission; a reason for being here. The details of each person's path are different, but the importance of the mission is grand, and inside of each one of us, we know we are meant to create something special with our lives.

One of life's great discoveries is to find out who your hero is, and observe the traits or aspects that you most appreciate or love about that person. What may surprise you is that the things you admire in your hero are often the very things you deny about yourself.

Your hero reflects the parts of you that you are not yet expressing or are expressing in a form you have not acknowledged. Your hero is your mirror, teaching you about your own possibilities. The tears of inspiration that a hero brings to you are tears of recognition for yourself. If you are surprised by this notion, just look back at the heroes you had when you were little, and you'll see that something in you was just like those people. Just as it wasn't obvious to you then that you were like your hero, it's sometimes hard to see now that you are like your hero. But keep looking, and you'll eventually see it.

Think about some of the heroes who have inspired people by the thousands. I love to listen to Martin Luther King's speech "I have a dream." When I hear that speech, I become filled with purpose, strength, and awareness. There isn't a speck of uncertainty in my body or mind. I remember something about my life, my role, and my goals. I no longer feel tired or unguided. I feel clear and energized. I know I have a dream and I am motivated to pursue it.

One day, I decided to play his speech in a staff meeting. My entire staff was mesmerized by his words. They were teary-eyed and speechless. That afternoon, they answered the phone with renewed enthusiasm. They hugged patients, hugged each other, stayed late. . . Martin Luther King stayed with them all day — not the words, but something stronger than words. That speech touched the unsung heroes in each of them, and motivated them to express their own ideas of brotherhood, love, and unity.

A hero's inspiration is contagious because it awakens our own. When people say they are touched by heroic actions or words, they are saying that a hero reached out and shook their own sleepy hero awake. What you revere in your hero is your next experience waiting to find a place to happen. You are called upon to turn your life into more opportunity for inspiration — to be purposeful. Remember, inspiration isn't just about *being*. It's also about *doing*. Using your hero as your guide, you'll find that you can become inspired, clarify your life's mission, and move yourself into action. With your hero in your heart, you can push through your comfort zone and beyond your own perceived limitations.

# Your Hero Will Smooth Your Path

Think of the teachers who have been the most influential in your life. Their students paid attention, participated, and gave more effort to finish homework assignments. The mood of the classroom was light and the atmosphere was easy, even when the work was difficult. Heroes are those kinds of people. They are the people who help you to be present, stimulate your mind, touch your heart, and make you want to accomplish something. Your hero is your greatest teacher.

Inspiration doesn't come from the brain. It comes from the heart. Our greatest teachers — our heroes — don't make us *think* we can get through something. They make us know we can. They give us that gift. And like any true gift, it comes from the heart and is accepted in the heart. Our heroes concentrate every cell of their bodies on their goal, mission or purpose — no matter what. We admire them because we feel the intensity of their inspiration. We resonate with their experience and it becomes a sort of accomplishment for us, too. A hero gives us our first taste of reaching our own pinnacle of success. That gift is one that becomes part of us, and that we take forward in our lives.

People can tell us to keep our chins up, and assure us that we can overcome obstacles. But encouraging words pale in comparison to the example our heroes set. When we see them go through something that we dread or fear, or achieve success in the face of incredible odds, our heart opens and new strength flows in.

We all know and understand the expression "He just didn't have the heart to keep going." And we've all encountered dark forests and storms on our life's path that made us wonder if we had the heart to keep moving. Sometimes the true test of our commitment is just that: to forge ahead. That's all. Discouragement slows us down. Hopelessness kills our spirit. Fear saps us of our resolve. We can take hardship. What we cannot take is hardship without a hero. Our heroes inspire us to be courageous enough to look forward, hopeful enough not to give up, and strong enough to persist. Our heroes give us heart.

When I was 16 years old, working in a nursing home as an aide, I watched my supervisor, Brenda, rescue a woman from choking. The patient was colorless, gasping for air, her eyes wild with panic. It frightened me more than anything I had ever seen. Brenda walked up to her, lifted her, turned her around, and popped the "cork" right out. She did it with confidence, concern, and without causing any extra panic. She knew she could help. She was laser-quick. And she was my hero. "That was close," she said. While I was still shaking from nerves, she was onto her next task. I admired her cool handling of the situation — her absolute certainty about what to do — and I wanted to be like that. It was one of my first realizations of knowing what I wanted to do in my life.

Over the years, I have been exposed to many traumatic situations, first as a nurse's aide, then as a nurse, and now as a doctor. I have become increasingly skilled at helping people handle health crises. While Jared gained strength from Arnold, the Terminator, my certainty about what to do came from a composite of my heroes — the people who successfully handled scary situations. Many times in my life I had watched in admiration as one person magically transformed a disaster into a miracle, and I yearned to be able to do that. And, there I was, during a walk in the park on a Sunday afternoon, meeting Jared, the little messenger who helped me learn that I really can do what I love to do. I have had the capacity to do it all along.

I wonder what path Jared will pursue in his life. He has only begun his journey of discovering himself through his heroes. I am certain that they will be with him as he finds his inspirations and takes the action steps to live his dreams. Just as my heroes are with me. Just as your heroes are with you.

### *Your Hero Tells You About Yourself*

Everyone has at least one hero. Here are some questions to help you identify yours:

Who do you look up to?

Who do you admire?

Who do you like to listen to?

Who do you feel innately proud of?

Who do you love to hear about?

Who gives you hope?

Who makes you catch yourself saying, "That's amazing!"

Who brings a tear of joy to your eyes?

Who has turned a disaster into a miracle?

## *That's your hero.*

Once you've identified your hero, you'll know more about yourself, because your hero is reflecting you.

\* \* \* \* \* \*

In Chapter Ten, you will learn the secrets to teaching with wisdom.

# About Dr. Amelia Case

Amelia Webber Case, D.C., a licensed chiropractic physician, is the founder of Universal Health Institute, a multidisciplinary natural health care center in Chicago. Dr. Case opened her private practice in 1990, and has transformed her single doctor office into a unique organization of like-minded doctors and therapists. Universal Health Institute is a place where people seeking natural health care options can count on a blend of traditional and alternative methods joining to offer non-drug and non-surgical intervention for any type of health problem.

Dr. Case is also a teacher, and she frequently travels throughout North America and Europe presenting lectures to chiropractic and medical students, as well as her own community in Chicago. In addition to her background in human anatomy, physiology, and natural health care, she is a long time student of philosophy, physics, comparative religion, and history, and brings her love of these subjects into her teaching and private practice.

She is certified to teach the work of Dr. John F. Demartini, the creator of The Breakthrough Experience™ seminar, and is ranked as a Gold Medal Trainer for one-on-one personal coaching by the Concourse of Wisdom School of Philosophy and

Healing. Dr. Case aims to expand her proficiency to help people achieve healthy, prosperous, and fulfilling lives by constantly improving her communication and coaching skills.

Dr. Case says, "The human body is always talking to us, in one way or another, asking for alignment. It's called many different things — equilibrium, poise, evenness — but I like the words balance and alignment. If we appreciate the body enough to listen, and answer the call to change what causes imbalance, then we will have a body that operates in a most efficient and healthy state; that's when we're really able to live and shine as human beings. I will learn and use every tool I can find to help people return to health. Then they have the opportunity to experience life as inspiring and rewarding."

# Universal Health Institute
*A Unique Approach to Healing*
8 West Chestnut
Chicago, Illinois 60610
312-266-9090

At Universal Health Institute, a unique combination of traditional and alternative health care methods are used to provide relief from pain and to revitalize the body from fatigue, stress, and chronic illness. Safe, reliable treatments such as chiropractic, kinesiology, holistic medicine, nutrition, exercise therapy, physical and massage therapy, craniosacral therapy, acupuncture, and personal coaching are used to help stop pain, restore normal function, and revitalize life.

Under the direction of Chief-of-Staff, Dr. Amelia Case, licensed, experienced, and certified doctors and therapists use their skills to help return the human body to its normal healthy state so that people can live more prosperous and fulfilling lives. The constant pursuit to sharpen the staff's focus and energy toward the patients is an important goal at Universal Health Institute. Time-honored healing methods such as prayer, meditation, humor, music, aromatherapy, and touch are added to high-tech diagnostics and modern treatment strategies to supplement and improve care programs. The team at Universal Health Institute is dedicated to learn, master, and apply high-quality natural health care that revolves around helping people to heal from the inside out, and to avoid needless surgery or unnecessary drugs.

"Health care isn't just about repairing a problem. It's about co-ordinating the body's functions, and transforming life from one stage to another," Dr. Case teaches her staff. "It isn't just the physical body that seeks balance and alignment. The chemical and mental aspects of the human body possess a natural urge to move in that direction, too. All we have to do is recognize and harness that impulsion, and our birthright — health — is available. The human body is the instrument we use to express our divine potential, and that potential can be best expressed through a tool well cared for. The best care we can give to ourselves and our patients is to find a way to balance the forces that challenge the physical, chemical, and mental aspects of our bodies."

---

## CHAPTER TEN

# Teaching with Wisdom

*by*
*Karrin Ochoa*

# Teaching with Wisdom

### Karrin Ochoa

*"If a teacher loves a child and gives
that child a love of the subject then
nothing more is necessary."*

– Glen Doman,
*How to Teach Your Baby to be Physically Superb*

To teach children the power of unconditional love, by your example, is the greatest teaching that you can offer. For children to know that they are unconditionally loved, whether they exceed your expectations or fall short, is the greatest gift you can give them. You never know when the things you teach a child will take hold. Children learn in their own perfect timing.

When it comes to teaching important principles, be sure to use plenty of repetition. Teach kids that fear and guilt are temporary, but love is forever. Empower kids by guiding them to their own solutions. Know and communicate that life is fair and everything happens for a reason. Share inspiring stories about amazing people who have overcome obstacles. If your child feels that they or someone else is a victim, you can guide them by asking questions that make them aware of opportunities within difficult situations.

Help children through transitions by waking them up to their responsibilities. Show them how to divide lifelong dreams into manageable pieces. Pull back the reins when they're under the delusion that they're invincible. Be present with them when they are tuning out. Encourage kids to think twice and act with confidence. Get used to hearing, "You're no fun!" and "Thanks so much." Kids are as contrary as anyone else. Be flexible. We all have the right to change our minds.

Teach that moderation is more powerful than going to extremes. Every up has its down and every high has its low in this world. Use knowledge to motivate. Read, read, read, and then read some more. Teach, by example, to focus on what you love. Know what is important to each child. Suggest, more than demand. Listen and see the big picture before taking action. Delegate and follow through. Reprimand with certainty and equally praise them without hesitation. Most importantly, make it a top priority to surround children with wise people and a quality environment.

Know that:

➤ Every child is here to express his or her own magnificence.

➤ Human beings, no matter what age, are not entirely guilty or completely innocent.

➤ In their own unique way, children will do everything you have done, just as you will do everything your parents did.

➤ Loving your own childhood and appreciating your upbringing will maximize your potential to influence your children with love.

➤ The people you love are designed to open you up and shut you down the most.

➤ Caring for children means entering the land of no excuses.

# A Parent's Biggest Challenge

*"If there is anything that we wish to change in the child,*
*we should first examine it and see whether it is not*
*something that could better be changed in ourselves."*

– Carl Jung

Parents can feel especially challenged when they discover that their child is doing or not doing something that they don't like about themselves. As a parent, you will overreact when a child does things that you judge either negatively or positively. For example, if you were bitten by a dog as a child and are still afraid of dogs, you will overreact when any dog approaches your child. Children are designed to attract the very things that their parents haven't loved. This is a magnificent opportunity for you to examine past events that you once judged and learn to see them as genuinely worthwhile experiences.

Everything you judge about yourself or others will eventually resurface, presenting you with another opportunity to deal with the issue. Perhaps the blessings within your judgments are not obvious at first glance, yet with self-reflection you will discover how they serve you. Once you come to know that your biggest challenges taught you the most, you can communicate this to your child with the wisdom that you have gained.

You serve your child well by asking quality questions and holding your child accountable to their own dreams. Remember that no child can skip steps in their journey, yet they can learn in days what took you years to realize.

A child will open up to you when they believe that you will listen without judgment. Your child will develop more perseverance and patience if they are aware that all people encounter pleasure and pain throughout their life. As a wise parent, do not rescue your child's desperation, but assist your child in discovering their own creative ways to get where they would love to go. Every time your child overcomes an obstacle, their self-worth increases. As their self-worth grows, they become better at identifying and communicating their values and purpose to others. Their desire to grow will be ignited and many opportunities will come their way.

If you are waiting until your child deserves respect by showing you respect, you are playing a silly game. Thinking that you are right and your child is wrong will only exaggerate the problem. Perhaps, up until now, you haven't had the tools to help you get past your own emotions that cause you to judge your child. Personal judgment is the only thing that creates distance in any relationship. As you realize that trying to fix your child doesn't work, you will stop blaming him or her for your reactions. Loving relationships begin with people loving each other as they are.

# Insightful Questions

*"Every child has a right to its own bent. It has a right to find its own way and go its own way, whether that way seems wise or foolish to others, exactly as an adult has."*

– George Bernard Shaw

1.   Are the majority of the activities that you do with and for your child things that you love to do or things that you have to do?

2.   When it's time to have a talk with your child, is there usually something wrong, or do you regularly take time to talk because you enjoy hearing what your child has to say?

3.   Are your expectations for your child based on who they are and their value systems, or on what you think they should be?

4.  Does your child spontaneously express their love and appreciation to you, or are your displays of affection more or less routine?

5.  Have you clearly identified what it is you would love to teach your child and set up a plan of action that is producing the results that you desire, or are you relying on other people to educate your child?

6.  Do you and your child know what each other's top values are, or do you expect your child to have the same belief system as you?

These questions are designed to clarify your aspirations as a parent and teacher. They remind us that every child who feels judged wilts, while children who feel unconditionally loved bloom. Children are one of life's ultimate gifts. They are born with unlimited potential and deserve the best we have to offer. Raising children takes an enormous vision, non-wavering commitment, and infinite energy.

# Self-Reflection is the Answer

*"It is not a guiding spirit that reveals to me secretly in a flash what I must say or do, but thought and reflection."*

– William H. Herndon and Jesse W. Weik

Self-reflection is the art of seeing the big picture and finding the hidden order when chaos is all that seems to exist. Self-reflection is not a pleasure-seeking, instant gratification answer. It's about vulnerability, responsibility, and wisdom. Parents who take the time to see that their children are mirrors of themselves learn a great deal from their kids. Great leaders are often masters of self-reflection. The primary reflection that children thrive upon is the reflection of unconditional love. A parent who practices the art of self-reflection, has a child who feels understood, valued, and unconditionally loved. Children learn by example that when a parent opens their heart to them, their heart automatically opens too. Problems dissolve when people open their hearts and minds to the wisdom of love.

As you practice the art of self-reflection you will awaken to find that:

➤ Your children are absolutely magnificent and totally lovable just as they are.

➤ Your gratitude for the opportunity to be a parent increases by discovering the wisdom in your parenting style, which increases your overall self worth.

➤ You *do* know what to do. A clear and inspired plan of action that will ultimately serve the entire family will be revealed to you.

## Family Dynamics

*"The family requires the most delicate mixture of
nature and convention, of human and divine,
to subsist and perform its function."*
– Allan Bloom, *The Clean Slate*

Family dynamics can be overwhelming and confusing until you've learned the universal dynamics that govern them. Understanding and discovering universal dynamics within families can transform the "craziest" family into one that is perfectly functioning and really quite amazing. Family relationships are the foundation upon which all other relationships are built. How you feel about your family members is a direct reflection of how you feel about yourself and others. Respect and appreciation for the varied and diverse personality traits of each family member in relationship to each other is vital for your well being.

Every person in the family ultimately reflects and balances every other person. For example, you won't find a "black sheep" or difficult child without a "white sheep" or good child. It's enlightening to know that the "difficult" child is outwardly expressing the "good" child's inner world and vice versa. Even more magnificent is the realization that the entire family unit expresses every aspect of each individual in the family. Although people express themselves uniquely, each member has every trait that every other family member has. This applies whether the connection between people is genetic or not. People don't have to live with one another, or even be alive in order for a relationship to exist. It is quite possible that a deceased or estranged family member has more influence on the family than the people who are interacting together on a daily basis.

Families come in countless variety, yet the purpose of a family is to give each person an opportunity to expand their potential through equal doses of support and challenge as they learn to love. People who do what they are inwardly called to do, know that at times they will go it alone, and at other times they will depend on others. A fine balance between dependence and independence is especially important in parent/child relationships. Anyone who feels called to a particular mission knows the importance of tuning into something greater than himself or herself. Since the family, as a whole, is larger than the sum of its parts, each family member is given, from day one, the opportunity to participate in something larger than they are. Every person has a responsibility to discover his or her own purpose. Nobody knows another person's purpose, we only know our own. Opportunities that allow us to explore and discover more of "who we are" are priceless. Children and adults have a universal desire to experience the freedom that comes from living their life on purpose.

# The Giant Juggling Act

*"Pursue some path, however narrow and crooked,*
*in which you can walk with love and reverence."*

– Henry David Thoreau

Every person in the family has multiple areas in their lives requiring attention. Some of these areas will be more of a priority than other areas, depending on the person. No area is better or worse than any other area. People who get along best in this world have a balance among every area of life. Spirituality, in its multitude of forms, is universal among the people of the world. Spiritual experiences are designed to open our hearts and minds. The moments that give our existence meaning are filled with gratitude, unconditional love, and awe. These inspired experiences are the doorways to each individual's soul-inspired purpose.

Brilliant people have an awareness of their purpose in life and are able to chunk it down and pursue it. A desire for life-long learning and education is a top priority for a brilliant mind. Mental clarity makes life interesting. All human beings thrive with a balance of outer stimulation and the opportunity to explore their inner wealth of creativity. The brain develops by use. The mind expands through the integration of knowledge and balanced perception. An environment that enables children to have moderate habits and develop unique talents is essential for learning and well-being.

Superior nutrition is also essential because it influences a child's entire physical, mental, and emotional health. Moderating blood sugar, eating regular nutritious meals, and drinking plenty of pure water all assist people in having a consistent high level of energy every day. As kids develop the habits that show respect for their physical body, they naturally participate in physical activities that they genuinely enjoy. When the body is in balance, it resonates at a high vibration, which assists in attracting magnificent opportunities.

Having the self-worth to do what one loves to do is one of the greatest opportunities there is. Exposure to the universal laws of financial mastery is a potential treasure box of wealth. An organized financial practice takes one far in life. The ability to earn and wisely manage one's money can be taught at any age. It's never too early or late to begin to practice the laws of fair exchange, saving, and investing. Families who manage their resources wisely often share fundamental common values while still remaining unique as individuals. They tend to have greater levels of appreciation for each other and a more powerful influence in their community.

Another aspect of teaching with wisdom is showing your children how to appreciate many different people and cultures, so they can expand their horizons. Those who have insight into other people's lives can connect with them on common ground. Those who learn to connect and provide a service for others have more expansive networks. As children learn to equally give and receive, their integrity shines through.

Balancing all of these areas of life through awareness and organization takes effort. People who put attention on their highest priorities are filled with energy and light.

Look and see if every family member's schedule includes a balance of the following:

➤ Career and/or school

➤ Nutritious food and exercise

➤ Money management

➤ Spiritual practice

➤ Family events and responsibilities

➤ Friends and play

➤ Personal talents

People who do what they love, enjoy life. It's when people feel like they *have to* do certain things that life feels like a burden. The difference between loving an activity and resenting it is the meaning that we give it. Learning to identify individual values and linking activities to those values makes us more willing to take on responsibility. When people are grateful for the opportunity to participate in an activity, they become more focused, creative, and on target. The key to being able to manage so many interests with abundant energy is to have enthusiasm and love for each activity.

Enthusiastic teachers have enthusiastic students. Wise teachers look for the spark of inspiration in their students' eyes. They know that every child is born to bring to life the wondrous visions that they see. When parents acknowledge and nurture their child's brilliance they give him or her a gift that will be passed on for generations. Teachers and parents who put their hearts and minds into raising soul-inspired children are enlightened with an overflow of love for kids. Children who know they are valued live life with an inner enthusiasm that lights up the world.

\*  \*  \*  \*  \*  \*  \*

In Chapter Eleven, discover the blessings of misfortune.

# About Karrin Ochoa

Karrin Ochoa is a professional parent, teacher, and author of numerous books and workshops. She is certified as a Professional Parent through the Institute for the Achievement of Human Potential and has home-schooled her four children for nineteen years. She has been the director of a private nursery school, a nanny, a child care provider, and a tutor.

Karrin is also a Counselor of Wisdom, certified with the Concourse of Wisdom School of Philosophy and Healing, based in Houston, Texas. Her mission is to teach universal principles to children and adults while applying them to her own life. Her purpose is to love unconditionally and inspire others to do the same. In honor of her dedication and her outreach of love and wisdom throughout the world, Dr. John F. Demartini, creator of The Breakthrough Experience™ and founder of the Concourse of Wisdom, presented her with the Ambassador of Wisdom award.

Karrin has extensive experience working with children. She facilitated summer camp for kids, hosted nine foreign exchange students, has been the leader of fifteen scouting troops for boys and girls, a coach of youth sports, and an author and facilitator of dozens of workshops for children and adults. She also structured and teaches The Breakthrough Experience™ seminar for Children.

As an inspired teacher, Karrin is dedicated to her continued study and research into a variety of disciplines that span her interests and areas of expertise.

She has studied thousands of books in numerous fields of interest such as childcare and development, nutrition, leadership, philosophy, religion, and science.

# Karrin Ochoa

4641 Magens Bay
Oceanside, Ca. 92057

760-721-1031
email: ochoa7@home.com

Karrin Ochoa teaches universal principles to children and adults through her books, seminars and workshops. She is also available for private coaching and consulting, either in person or by phone.

## Books Include:

### *Everyday Wisdom*

A quote a day with quality questions and activities to motivate and uplift you. Its amazing how problems dissolve and opportunities arise as you apply a little bit of *Everyday Wisdom* every day.

### *777 Words to Collapse—On your journey to unconditional love*

This book is exclusively for those who have completed The Quantum Collapse Process™ with a certified Counselor of Wisdom. The book will assist you to completely collapse issues and experience signs of illumination. Buy it, use it, and watch your life magnificently unfold before your eyes.

# Seminars Include:

## The Breakthrough Experience™

The Breakthrough Experience™ will totally shift your perceptions and raise your consciousness. This life-altering, two-day course features The Quantum Collapse Process™ and profound Universal Principles. The Breakthrough Experience™ is the first in a series of courses offered through The Concourse of Wisdom School of Philosophy and Healing.

Karrin Ochoa has been teaching The Breakthrough Experience™ to both adults and children for several years. Prior to facilitating this seminar, she devoted five years of her life to the daily research and study of the principles and philosophies included in The Breakthrough Experience™.

## Transformation

This one-day course offers each student the opportunity to experience The Quantum Collapse Process™ This process is one of the few scientific tools that are guaranteed to literally raise your energy and vibration. Every time you complete a Collapse, you illuminate your life and strengthen your connection to your soul.

## Children's Breakthrough

Kids who participate in the Children's Breakthrough Program experience:

➢ A solid foundation in understanding universal laws (Yes, children can and do learn advanced concepts from the fields of physics, philosophy, and health.)

➢ Exercises to challenge the mind and open the heart (100% joy-based activities)

➤ Discipline, self-mastery, and accountability

➤ Increased self-worth

➤ Lessons they will remember for the rest of their lives

## The Genius is Awake

Your genius awakens in direct proportion to your acknowledgment of your own magnificence. This half-day program will confront your excuses and make you accountable to your own dreams. Turn up your enthusiasm for life by attending The Genius is Awake.

## Family Dynamics

There is a hidden order underlying the dynamics that run every family. This fascinating 6-week workshop will provide you with the tools to solve conflicts, dissolve childhood issues, and understand the perfection in your relationships. You will open your heart and feel tremendous gratitude for your family.

## Leadership Programs for Teens

A variety of programs for teens are offered from one-day motivational and goal setting programs to six-week programs that provide accountability and long term progress. Individual counseling is also available for teens. Teens will learn how to:

➤ Increase their energy and interest in living

➤ Overcome obstacles

➤ Understand and appreciate themselves and others

➤ Learn quick decision-making techniques

➤ Challenge themselves physically and mentally

➤ Identify their dreams

## Teacher and Parent Training

These workshops are available on evenings and weekends throughout the year. Workshops vary in length from the shortest being a few hours and the longest meeting once a month for eight months.

Topics include:

➤ The Art of Inspired Teaching

➤ Cutting Edge Motivation and Organizational Secrets

➤ Nourishing Bright Students

➤ Transforming ADD-ADHD

➤ Curriculum training

➤ Universal principles

Karrin also custom-designs seminars and workshops to meet the specific goals of individuals and organizations.

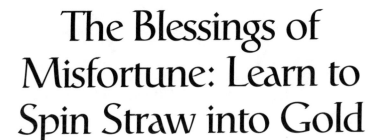

# CHAPTER ELEVEN

## The Blessings of Misfortune: Learn to Spin Straw into Gold

*by*
*Christine K. Clifford*

# The Blessings of Misfortune: Learn to Spin Straw into Gold

## Christine K. Clifford

---

*"Success is to be measured not so much by the position that one has reached in life as by the obstacles which he has overcome while trying to succeed."*

– Booker T. Washington

---

Are there things in your life which you've always wanted to experience; however, for a wide variety of reasons (expense, time, geography, practicality, fear, etc.), you've never gotten around to doing them? Suddenly, adversity comes into your life and you think to yourself, *now I'll never be able to have that experience or fulfill my dreams.*

Crisis and misfortune can cripple an individual's goals and aspirations in a heartbeat, or it can be the stepping stone to reevaluate your priorities and life dreams, providing the catalyst to make your dreams come true.

# How People Feel When They Face Adversity and Undergo Change in Their Lives

Each and every one of us has had to face some sort of adversity in our lifetime, be it illness, divorce, loss of employment, the death of a loved one, financial hardship, or environmental catastrophes. Quite often we don't have the ability to change that "thing" that is going on in our lives.

Unfortunately, what's inside most individuals who are dealing with misfortune is a lot of negative emotions: anger, fear, denial, confusion, and grief. But the one thing we *can* change and do something about, is our *attitude*, and how we choose to deal with that adversity on a "go forward" basis.

## Channel Feelings of Sorrow and Grief into Life-Affirming Changes

The year I turned 40, my life was going beautifully. My husband and I celebrated our twentieth wedding anniversary. We had two healthy, active boys ages 11 and 8. I was just completing the most successful year of my 15-year career as a senior executive vice president of an international marketing services company, having recently signed the largest contract in the history of our industry. My husband and I were a month away from submitting an offer on the house of our dreams. I was on top of the world.

Then, in a matter of minutes, my life came to a screeching halt. I found a lump in my breast while doing a routine self-exam. My mother had died an untimely death at the age of 42 from breast cancer. Although three different doctors told me I didn't have cancer, I finally convinced my gynecologist to do a needle biopsy. Four days later, my fears were confirmed and I was scheduled for surgery. I cried for three days without stopping.

My parents were the only people I knew who had dealt with a diagnosis of cancer, and unpropitiously, they didn't have the strength to be positive role models. When my mother received her test results, she sank into a deep, clinical depression, which rendered her unable to function with the simplest tasks of everyday living. My father, a prestigious physician, unable to deal with her depression, left her.

All I could think of when I heard the words, "I'm so sorry, Christine, you have cancer," was "I'm going to get depressed, my husband is going to leave me, and I'm going to die." The last thing on earth I expected was that this life-size adversity would prove to be a gift: the gift of life and the springboard for living my dream.

## Jumping Off the Treadmill

As much as I loved my busy job at the marketing company, the stress of constant travel, combined with the growing pains of expanding our business, raising a family, and being a wife had become overbearing. I had very little free time to pursue my hobbies and on top of it all, I had a life-threatening disease, which I knew would take every ounce of energy I had.

From the time I was a young girl, I had dreamt of becoming an author. My writing skills were left to training manuals, memos, minutes, and the occasional "white paper," but whenever people read what I wrote ("thank you notes" were my specialty), they would always say, "Christine, you should be a writer."

I heard the phrase so frequently that I thought long and hard about why I had never pursued my passion. The same answer always floated to the top of my list: I couldn't think of a subject that I felt I knew enough about to put a pen to paper.

Six weeks after my cancer surgery, I awoke in the middle of the night with a vision: cartoons. I made my way through the dark downstairs to our family room, and as I sat at my desk, as many as 50 cancer-related cartoons flowed into my head. I scribbled madly, sketching and writing punch lines, until exhausted, I crept back to bed, pulled the covers up to my chin, and thought to myself, "What was that?"

Days, weeks, months passed by as I trudged on through my treatments. My cartoons and "my book" became my focus as I searched for signs of humor in my predicament. The harder I looked, the more I found, and my first book *Not Now...I'm Having a No Hair Day!* was born.

# Embrace Your Adversity as a Gift That Allows You Permission to Make Changes and Pursue Your Dream

Exactly one year from the day I sat in the hospital recovering from cancer surgery, I sat in a publisher's office and signed a contract for not one, but two books about using humor as a tool to deal with a diagnosis of cancer. My books launched a secondary career as a professional speaker as organizations and associations started hiring me to help them find the humor in their life challenges and misfortunes.

I had openly shared my cartoons and developing books with my employer, family, and friends who quickly realized that these cartoons and books had become my therapy. They were the focus I needed to propel me toward recovery and find that "positive attitude."

I literally embraced my disease, and because it had such a life-affirming quality to it, those around me chose to embrace the changes as well. When my writing and speaking finally became more than a "full time job," I was able to leave the marketing company gracefully with their encouragement, support, best wishes, confirmation, and permission, knowing that while one door was closing, a new one was being opened...

# Research All of the Possibilities: Prepare Your Dream for Change

I can clearly remember the reactions I received when I first started sharing my cartoons and my developing "book" with other people. I could see the wheels spinning 'round in their heads, thinking to themselves, "Isn't it great that Christine has found something to focus on that is helping her get through this experience. But a book?! Fat chance *that* will ever become a reality!"

Despite the reactions of "doubting Thomas's," I carried my cartoons/book with me everywhere I went. Any chance I had to share it with someone, I would in the hope they might know someone or something that could help make my vision a reality.

# Document Your Dream to Make It a Reality

If you believe strongly enough in yourself, your company, your product, or your cause, anything is possible. I boarded an airplane in Detroit heading for Minneapolis on one of the few business trips I took on behalf of the marketing company the year I was going through my cancer treatments and trying to make my dream a reality. Luck would have it that I sat down in first-class right next to the number one news anchor in Minneapolis, who was returning from a hot story. Luck has been defined as "when preparation meets opportunity," and when she started asking me how I was doing with my cancer treatments, I pulled my cartoons out of my briefcase and showed them to her.

Unbeknownst to me, the anchor had lost her only sister to cancer at the age of 35. Cancer was a subject near and dear to her heart. She laughed out loud at my amateur work and said, "Christine, we simply have to do a story on this." Now I was really committed to my dream!

## Create a Niche to Fulfill Your Dream

I started to research the possibilities of making my dream a reality by visiting the public library, bookstores, and the Internet for other humorous books about cancer. I quickly learned that there was limited material about my dream, which confirmed for me that there was an unfulfilled need.

Webster defines "niche" as a place or position precisely suited to a person's talents. Take the broad base of your dream and ask yourself:

➤ Can I offer something or have I done something unique that no one (or few people) has done before?

➤ Is there an area of my dream that is untapped or unfulfilled?

➤ Do I have much competition?

➤ Can I put a new twist on my subject matter that will appeal to a broad range of people?

Whatever your misfortune or challenge is, solve it, and you can sell it to the world. Allow your problem to become your strength.

## Market Your Dream Like Crazy!

Once you acquire the knowledge, skills, and techniques to generate your dream, it's time to expand beyond your immediate situation. Leave no stone unturned in making your dream a reality. The news anchor ran the story about my dream: a six-minute piece that aired on the 10 p.m. news. I hadn't even found a publisher for my book, but the community soon learned that I was now an author! There was no turning back.

I began to develop professional tools that would help me "market" my dream. I designed brochures and hand-outs about my work and my cartoons, developed bookmarks that were unique and memorable, and created a web site to promote my dream. I also began to establish credibility in a related field (healthcare) by joining industry-related associations, writing articles for newspapers and magazines, and collecting letters of recommendation from experts in my new field.

# Incorporate Your Dream into Everyday Reality

Once you've made the firm decision to move forward with your dream or vision, say it out loud. Write it down. Shout it from the rooftops until everyone you know is sharing in that vision. Too many of us keep our dream a secret — afraid of the ridicule, rejection, confusion, or misunderstandings that we perceive may be out there. But once you've committed to your dream, there is nowhere to go but forward.

The same news anchor who helped me launch my dream came upon her own misfortune when several years later, she underwent a series of eye surgeries that rendered her unable to perform her tasks on air. While struggling to come to grips with what she would do with the rest of her life, a magazine article quoted her as stating that she wanted to raise $1 million to endow a chair in her physician's name at a local University Medical School.

Once she documented her dream, and began sharing it, all kinds of opportunities presented themselves and doors began to open. A professional fund-raiser who used to live next-door to the physician called the anchor and volunteered to chair her fund-raiser. Dozens of members of the community and contacts from the anchor's professional and personal friendships came forth with offers of support.

> *"What you can do, or dream you can, begin it;*
> *Boldness has genius, power and magic in it."*
>
> – Johann Wolfgang von Goethe

## Pursue Your Dream with "Baby Steps"

Most of us don't have the resources to drop everything we're doing in pursuit of our life dreams, especially if we're dealing with adversity or misfortune. Pat yourself on the back for the accomplishments you've made while dealing with your challenge. Set small goals and deadlines that will move you forward without totally abandoning your responsibilities and commitments. Reward yourself when breakthroughs present themselves and remind yourself that "Rome wasn't built in a day." Celebrate every victory.

## Focus on Your Dream and the Positive Attitude it Brings Back into Your Life

There comes a time in most people's lives when they accept that challenges and misfortunes happen to us all. Many people speak of the gifts and privileges that misfortune has brought their way and are grateful for those gifts and life lessons. The realization that you can actually live your dream is the greatest gift of all. Cherish the positive, life-affirming qualities that overtake every aspect of your being — your heart, your body, your mind, and your soul — when you can truly say, "I'm living my dream."

# Breakthrough Dreaming: Spin Straw into Gold

Eventually you will realize that it's time to take that "leap of faith" to start living your dream. As hard as it is to abandon the comfort and security of your present life, opening the door to your vision will ultimately bring you to an even more fulfilling place.

I'm a firm believer that good things happen to good people. When you are in the midst of a crisis or catastrophe in your life, you can't imagine how you will ever get through it and find "life" on the other side. Your life may never be the same because of that experience, but that doesn't mean you can't have a good life, a better life, a productive life, the life of your dreams.

## Use the Media to Gain Notoriety and Grow Your Dream

Once you've made that "leap of faith," use the media to gain recognition and acceptance of your dream. Think of all the small, local periodicals and newspapers you can contact: your high school, college, fraternity/sorority, church or synagogue, hometown newspaper, health club newsletter, etc. Send them a simple, one-page press release of how you are living your dream, how it helped you get through your adversity, and how it's changed your life. The media is always looking for stories of success and inspiration.

## Remember Your Adversity and Give Back to the Community

I made two promises to myself seven years ago: If I lived, I would find something that would bring meaning to my life, while continuing to support my family. I found that meaning with the creation of my new life as an author, speaker, and business owner. My second promise was that once I found that "meaning in my life," I would do whatever I could to help the world find a cure for cancer.

As an avid golfer, with many connections throughout the golfing industry, I knew I could convey the passion and drive necessary to run a successful fund-raising event. Our 1998 inaugural event raised over $100,000 — 50 percent more than our targeted goal — making our donation the "most successful first-year event in the history of the American Cancer Society." I will eventually raise one million dollars for research to help find that cure.

Don't wait until catastrophe strikes your life before you make a decision to give something back. The rewards you will receive from the accomplishments of making a difference will far exceed other awards.

# Reaffirm Your Inner Voice and Live Your Dream

*"Let us be of good cheer, remembering that the misfortunes hardest to bear are those which never come."*

– Amy Lowell

I look back on the many roles I have played in my life: daughter, sister, student, wife, mother, businesswoman, entrepreneur, professional speaker, friend, volunteer, cancer survivor. But the role that I hold dearest to my heart and the one that fills me with pride is the role of my dreams: that of "author." Today is the perfect time to dream....

\* \* \* \* \* \*

In Chapter Twelve, learn how to get to the core of who you truly are.

# About Christine K. Clifford

**B**efore her bout with breast cancer, Christine Clifford had definitely cracked the glass ceiling. At the age of 40, she was Senior Vice President for SPAR Marketing Services, an international information and merchandising services firm based in Minneapolis, Minnesota.

Once the top salesperson in the billion dollar service industry, Christine was responsible for accounts with Kmart, Toys 'R' Us, Procter & Gamble, AT&T, Tyco Toys, and L'Oreal, among others.

Diagnosed with breast cancer in December of '94, Christine went on to write two award-winning portrayals of her story in her books, *Not Now...I'm Having a No Hair Day!* and *Our Family Has Cancer, Too!* written especially for children. Christine's third book, *Cancer Has Its Privileges*, will be published by Penguin Putnam in April 2002.

Christine is a contributing author to *Chicken Soup for the Survivor's Soul, Chicken Soup for the Golfer's Soul, Chicken Soup for the Writer's Soul,* and is featured in the book *The Courage to Laugh.*

Christine is currently President and Chief Executive Officer of THE CANCER CLUB®, a company designed to market humorous and helpful products internationally for people who have cancer. She serves as a spokesperson for HealthEast Care Systems and helped launch their new breast care center in May, 2000.

She has been featured in *Better Homes & Gardens, MORE* magazine, *American Health, Golf Digest, Today's Christian Woman,* as well as *The Singapore Women's Weekly* and the *Hindu* in India. Christine appeared on *CNN Live* as "one of the world's leading authorities on the use of therapeutic humor." She also appeared on Lifetime Television Network's *New Attitudes* show and the *Leeza Show.*

Host of *The Christine Clifford Celebrity Golf Invitational,* a benefit for breast cancer research, Christine's inaugural event raised over $100,000, making it the "most successful first-year event in the history of the American Cancer Society." She has received the *Council of Excellence* award for income development from the American Cancer Society.

Christine is a member of the Minnesota Speakers Association, the National Speakers Association, the American Association for Therapeutic Humor, and the National Association of Breast Cancer Organizations. She is listed in *International Who's Who of Professionals, International Who's Who of Entrepreneurs,* and *International Who's Who of Authors and Writers.* She is also listed in *Contemporary Authors* and *2,000 Notable American Women.*

She lives with her husband, John; sons, Tim and Brooks; and dog, Sneakers, in Edina, Minnesota.

# Christine K. Clifford

Humorist, Author, Professional Speaker
President/Chief Executive Officer of

## The Cancer Club®

6533 Limerick Drive
Edina, MN 55439
Phone: (952) 944-0639
Fax: (952) 941-1229
Email: Christine@cancerclub.com
Website: www.cancerclub.com

Christine is a victorious survivor, in business and in life, eagerly sharing her knowledge and combining her wisdom, humor, insight, and lifetime experiences. Christine guarantees that if you believe in yourself, your company, your product, or your cause, anything is possible!

Christine is available for seminars, workshops, and keynotes. Choose from lectures on marketing, media, change, inspiration, motivation, self-empowerment, recovery, and volunteerism. Christine addresses conventions, associations, women's events/ expos, healthcare focused events, the corporate arena, and all public and private sector organizations. Continuing Education credits are often available for Christine's programs.

# Programs Include:

➤ The Blessings of Misfortune:
Learn to Spin Straw into Gold

➤ From Road Warrior to Glorious Survivor

➤ Penny for Your Thoughts?
How to Start Your Business on a Shoestring Budget

➤ Am I Out of Sick Days Yet?

➤ ME, MYSELF & I: Market Yourself Like Crazy!

➤ Niche in a Nutshell:
Create a Market Only <u>You</u> Can Fill

➤ Use The Media to Gain Notoriety and
Grow Your Business

➤ Perfect the Art of Professional Begging:
Learn to Negotiate Donations for Yourself, Your
Company or Your Cause

# Books Include:

*Not Now...I'm Having a No Hair Day!*
(Pfeifer – Hamilton Publishers, Duluth, MN. 1996)

*Our Family Has Cancer, Too!*
(Pfeifer – Hamilton Publishers, Duluth, MN. 1998)

*Cancer Has Its Privileges: Stories of Hope & Laughter*
(Penguin Putnam, New York, NY. Due April 2002)

To place an order, call 1-800-586-9062 or visit
www.cancerclub.com.

**Don't forget to laugh!**™

## CHAPTER TWELVE

# Life is Like an Apple: Every Bite You Take Out of Life Brings You Closer to Your Core

*by*
*Lillian Zarzar*

# Life is Like an Apple: Every Bite You Take Out of Life Brings You Closer to Your Core

### Lillian Zarzar

---

*"The unexamined life is not worth living."*

– Socrates

---

What does it take to have the quality of life we desire? How much are we willing to sacrifice for the life we would love to live? Why are we here? What is the seed of our existence? How many bites must we take out of life before we find the inner core? Why are we sometimes afraid to seek our innermost essence?

The Orchard of Life beckons us to take the journey of a lifetime. As we walk our chosen path, we are provided with obstacles that both challenge and support us. As we pick the fruits offered, we have an obligation to examine each piece, determine its value to us, and assess how we may use it in service. Every opportunity serves others and us in some way.

Why is life like an apple? The apple is ubiquitous. It has been found on every continent and is known in every country. Its botanic origins are precisely unknown. However, from the Jordan River to the Tien Shan Valley of western China, from the Tigris and Euphrates to the Nile of Egypt, from Chile and Argentina to New England, apple trees have flourished. The Greeks, Romans, Russians, and Latin Americans have written poetry about them. The current word apple comes from the Old English "appel" which means "fruit." Interesting to note that in the story of Adam and Eve, the fruit referred to has usually been depicted as an apple. Sir Isaac Newton, himself, was inspired by the apple. Snow White was offered a poisonous apple. The apple in its many forms has existed for thousands of years. At this time, approximately 2,000 varieties of apples have been identified.

As we look at this universal fruit, we encounter similarities to our own existence and our journey through life. Apple trees follow watercourses and grow close to water sources. We all love to be near the water too. How many of us retreat and recreate at oceans, lakes, and rivers. The most expensive properties are often near the water, and when water isn't near, we build swimming pools and bring the water to us. The human body is composed mostly of water. We are baptized in water, we bless ourselves with it, and, like the apple, we not only want to live near it, we can't live without it.

The apple has a skin — so to get to the fruit inside, we have to penetrate or peel the outer layer. We have a skin, and as we learn about ourselves, we identify how "thick-skinned" or "thin-skinned" we are, don't we? And as we peel away our own layers, we gain greater awareness of ourselves. From the outside, the skin may be shiny, durable, and smooth, but we don't know what we will find inside. The apple may be appealing on the outside and "rotten to the core" within. Or, it might not look very pleasing on the outside, yet be filled with sweetness within. Appearances may betray what is inside.

Isn't life the same way? We expect life to go smoothly, to be in balance. Then we find that the road is rough and lopsided. We look at individuals and view how "attractive" they are on the "outside," yet find them "unattractive" on the "inside," or vice versa. How appropriate the popular adage, "You can't judge a book by its cover." Likewise, you can't tell the fruit of the apple by looking at it, and you can't predict life other than to know that you don't know what you will find along the way.

Upon examining the universal fruit of life, we find that:

Sometimes the fruit is crisp and succulent.

Sometimes the fruit is mushy and juiceless.

Sometimes the fruit tastes tart or sweet or bland.

Sometimes the fruit has a yellow tinge, bright white, or brown.

Sometimes the skin is bruised or firm or soft.

Isn't life much the same? We don't know what is inside until we explore and delve inside… by taking a bite.

The more we recognize that the whole of the apple, as well all of life, serves us in some way, the more meaningful our lives can be. There are four essential ingredients that can help us get to the CORE of who we are in understanding ourselves and leading a more fulfilling life. Getting to the CORE is a challenge because we don't always want to know what's inside of us. Are we afraid it might be mushy? Or too ripe? Is there a worm living within that we want to avoid? As we ponder the truth of our existence, let's examine the four essential elements that assist us in getting to the CORE: Courage, Omniscience, Resilience, Enthusiasm.

# Courage

The origin of the word courage comes from the Latin "cor" meaning "heart." Isn't it interesting that we talk about "getting to the heart of the matter," "speaking from the heart," or being "heartfelt" or "heartwarming?" We sing the lyrics "ya gotta have heart." The heart of the body pumps the lifeblood through the system. Without it, the system fails. The heart may represent love, honesty, sincerity, romance, fun, openness, essence, source, feeling, the list goes on. And remember the Lion in "The Wizard of OZ" desiring Courage? Consider King Richard as well — who was the "Lion-Hearted." A recent movie was titled "Braveheart."

To break the skin of the apple, to slice it open, takes courage. Life is risky, not knowing what lies ahead. *Yet the greater risk is taking none.* If we don't cut a slice or take a bite of the apple, we won't know what it tastes like. As Kahlil Gibran says, "your pain is the breaking of the shell that encloses your understanding." Courage involves facing new challenges, braving the elements, and confronting our fears. Courage means we make the decision to move forward, whether or not we know what will happen, because with each step we learn about our tenacity, our tolerance, and our toughness.

How did we learn all that we have acquired so far? We took a risk and learned how to walk, how to ride a bicycle, how to talk, how to drive, how to write our names. Everything we have ever learned involved the risk of taking the first step to do it. We learned that we could walk, and talk, and ride, and read, and write through constant "apple-cation." And it all starts with the risk of the first step. Without courage, we would still be crawling. With courage, we explore new avenues, new opportunities. The expression, "What have I got to lose?" puts risk into perspective. No matter what the risk, we obtain knowledge and awareness of our capabilities. Our courage builds confidence to persevere, and we thrive under challenging conditions.

# Omniscience

Omniscience stems from the Latin "omnis" meaning "all" and "scientia" being "knowledge." When we are born, a seed of awareness is planted in the heart of our souls. Blossoms of thoughts grow in our minds and the soul is our mind's gardener. We are born with a depth of understanding. It is our birthright.

Just because we can't communicate what we know as babies doesn't mean that we don't know. Like the seed of the apple containing the most concentrated nutrients and wisdom of the apple, so do our cell-seeds have an innate wisdom. The knowledge is contained in the seed. As the seed grows in its development, it's nurtured by the environment and surrounding elements. Everything attending to its awareness is used in its growth. That's why every experience, every bite, serves you. It's why your heart knows the truth of your existence. It is within the heart that we truly comprehend. Have you ever just had a feeling about something? Or perhaps you had a premonition, and the event came to pass?

Trust yourself. You know that you know. You have that feeling in your heart. You have that sense. When you try something new, it may be difficult at first, yet with practice, you learn. That foundation of learning builds through life and adds to your body of knowledge. When you trust what you know, you can better manage what you think you don't know. Every opportunity provides a fertile environment for growth and pruning.

The more you enhance your awareness, the less you are pushed and pulled by your emotions. With each bite of the apple, you branch out into areas you wouldn't have attempted. When you look back at the events in your life and can see the service provided for you and others, you see that in every benefit is a drawback and with every drawback is a blessing. Sometimes we realize it later. So while there may be tartness in the difficult lessons learned, there is promise as well of the sweetness of the fruit.

## Resilience

Your growth stems from the experiences you weather. As the apple tree blossoms under many challenging conditions, you blossom under the events that shape your life. The word "resilience" originates with the Latin "re" for "back" and "salire" meaning "leap." Your ability to bounce back from what you perceive as a debacle propels you onward. The more you can adapt to challenging conditions and brave the elements, the easier it is to thrive. Being resilient is also being multi-dimensional, being flexible.

An apple may be eaten raw or cooked as in a pie. It can be pureed into a sauce, processed into a spread, or pressed into cider. While the apple may take many forms, every morsel, just as every lesson in life, fortifies the body and mind with nutrients for growth. Myriad flavors and textures tantalize the palate. We seek to repeat the pleasures enjoying each bite. The pleasure of having what we want is fleeting, for what satisfies the body doesn't satisfy the soul. You are born for something greater and are endowed with the gifts to make it so.

Bend as the branches do in the storms of life, yet remain steady as the trunk of the tree withstands the pressure of the elements. Both flexibility and strength are necessary for growth. Take a chance and bloom with wisdom where you are. When we learn to appreciate all of life's opportunities as gifts in our evolution, we break through to a greater understanding of our existence.

## Enthusiasm

Passion is an essential ingredient of success. What are you willing to sacrifice to have what you would love? From the origin of the Greek "enthous" comes this word that denotes inspiration. Your passions and your inspirations are the source of your ability to create the life you desire. Opportunity comes in many forms. Just as there are hundreds of apple varieties, there are hundreds of ways for you to grow and achieve your success. Whatever you choose, do it with belief.

When our minds are balanced and our hearts are open, we know what we believe. Our belief is like a tiny sprout, which we water and nurture. We contemplate it. The messages of the soul provide impetus for the belief. What we accomplish in our passionate moments with the spirit of love and gratitude is inspiring. Our soul's purpose is inspiring. When we believe that we can, we do. When we imbue action with enthusiasm, we are unstoppable.

# The Core of the Human Spirit

What is *your* dream? You come into the Orchard of Life with the resources appropriate to realize your dreams. You are not given a dream you cannot live. The Universe doesn't make mistakes. The perfection of life is that our so-called "mistakes" are actually part of the growth process. You live your dreams when you have the courage to listen to the light of your soul speaking through your heart. Each inspired message is like a juicy apple, filled with sustenance and seeds of potential. When you listen to your soul's messages, you know.

Tap into the inner wellspring of your wisdom. Follow your lead, acknowledge your purpose. Be resilient to what the

Universe provides in challenge and support. You are here to make your mark of distinction. As you walk the path in the Orchard of Life, your light is passed on as a legacy of significance.

The next time you have an apple, slice it in half. If you slice it horizontally, you will see the shape of a heart around the seeds. When you slice it transversely, around the seeds is the shape of a star.

As you relish each bite of life, you are getting closer to your CORE. The Star of the apple represents Light and the Heart of the apple is Love. Isn't it evident, then, that the Core of who you are is, in essence, Love and Light? The closer you get to the core of who you are, the brighter you shine, and the greater your capacity to love and be loved.

# About Lillian Zarzar

Lillian Zarzar transfers principles that enhance self-awareness and improve productivity in your personal and professional life. She is an author, international speaker, and consultant who transforms people.

Lillian is the founder and owner of MIND*SHIFT*,™ a Columbus, Ohio based international company devoted to assisting individuals and organizations to shift perceptions, enhance inspirations, and increase awareness. She is the author of *Apple-osophy: Slices of Apple-Inspired Wisdom* and a co-author of *Breakthrough Secrets to Live Your Dreams*, and *Inspiring Breakthrough Secrets to Live Your Dreams*.

She is certified to teach The Breakthrough Experience,™ a seminar that helps you identify the spirit within and tap into the power available to you. Through the cutting-edge empowerment tool called The Quantum Collapse Process,™ Lillian teaches the principles of transformation.

Other presentations and seminars that she conducts include: *The CORE Principles of Empowerment, We Speak in Headlines, Communicating Through Conflict,* and *Take the Charge Out of Your Life.* Lillian is also available for personal consultations and small-group transformation sessions. Programs are customized to meet client needs.

Lillian has taken her message to the United Kingdom, Australia, South Africa, New Zealand, Ireland, and Southeast Asia. In her presence, participants receive the tools to take responsibility for self-enhancement in all areas of their lives.

For over ten years, Lillian has motivated and inspired her audiences to "get to the core" of who they are. She uses her theme of "apple-osophy" using the universal fruit, the apple, to help participants tap into a new way of *thinking beyond by going within* and shifting their lives.

**MIND*SHIFT***
...Transforming Lives

Lillian Zarzar transfers
Principles that enhance
self-awareness and improve
productivity in your professional
and personal life. She is an author,
international speaker, and consultant
who transforms people.

### *Consider the benefits:*

renewed sense of purpose
confidence to be assertive
process for conflict management
self-esteem enhancement
more productive approach to life
meaningful contribution to work

Her inspired yet practical message explores the metaphor of the universal fruit, the apple. She created the theme "Apple-osophy" for core courses in human development.

*"Lillian is an 'apple-osopher.' She has encouraged me to get to the core of who I am."*

– Margaret Hart Lewis

**"Get to the CORE"**
**Call Lillian Zarzar, MA**
**MIND*SHIFT***
**614-486-5523**
**email: applerose@columbus.rr.com**

# ACKNOWLEDGMENTS

Thank you to all of our significant others, family members, mentors, and friends who assisted in the creation and compilation of this book.

Thank you to Dr. John F. Demartini for taking the time out of his full schedule to write our foreword, and to The Concourse of Wisdom School of Philosophy and Healing for its ongoing support and challenge.

# SOURCES OF QUOTES

For kindly granting permission to reprint copyrighted material from the following books and CDs, the authors thank their respective publishers.

Paula Cole, "Me," on the CD, *This Fire*. Hingface Music, Los Angeles, CA.

Mark A. Lorenson, *Quotes for the Masters —The Sages' Secrets for Greater Life Mastery (Volumes I & II)*, Universal Consulting, Columbus, OH, 1999.

Ted Honderich, *The Oxford Companion to Philosophy*, Oxford University Press Inc. New York, NY, 1995.

Reader's Digest, *Quotable Quotes: Wit and Wisdom for all Occasions From America's Most Popular Magazine*, Reader's Digest Association, Inc., USA, 1997.

Every effort has been made to ensure that each author, songwriter, editor, and publisher has been properly acknowledged, although some sources were not traceable.

# JOURNAL YOUR DREAMS